"This is the book to show everyone that the past can't hold you down, that trauma can be overcome."

- MJ Caldwell, R.N.

"Living Hope is powerfully written and deeply mesmerizing. A must read for anyone seeking to shift their emotional pain to inner peace and emotional freedom. Lynne Cockrum-Murphy shares her compelling story so others may benefit."

- Connie M. Leach, ED.D , Career and Life Coach, author of *Adolescent Girls at Risk* and co-author of the *Charge up Your Life* books

Living Hope

STEPS TO LEAVING
SUFFERING BEHIND

LYNNE COCKRUM-MURPHY,
ED.D., L.I.S.A.C.

Lynne Cockrum-Murphy books are available for order
through Ingram Press Catalogues

Lynne Cockrum-Murphy
Visit my website at www.DesertJewel.org
www.LynneCockrum-Murphy.com

Printed in the United States of America

First Printing: August 2015
Published by Sojourn Publishing, LLC

ISBN: 978-1-62747-147-3
Ebook ISBN: 978-1-62747-148-0

Acknowledgement

E very day, when I wake up and again when I go to sleep at night, I express my gratitude for so much that gives me joy like these special people that enrich my life.

I want to thank my husband, Doug Murphy for all the ongoing support and unconditional love he has provided for thirty plus years. It certainly has changed my world view and life.

Also I deeply appreciate Tom Bird and his delightful team. He and RamaJon kindly guided me through the development of several books and encouraged me to share my story, strength and highest self.

I also acknowledge my amazing sister, Brenda Wodele, who allows me to put our family history (as I see it) into books. She is a loving supporter of my life.

And finally I thank all those unseen guides, masters, teachers and angels that are always actively involved, playing a nearly silent role in our lives yet rarely publicly acknowledged for all their unconditional love.

Prologue

I suspect you are attracted to this book because you have been in pain – emotional pain – and feel burdened by life's events and yet, you want so much more – and part of you believes it is possible.

Truth is it's more than possible. More than likely you chose this book, these steps, to propel yourself into the life you seek. Happiness comes to those who seek it and allow it.

Sharing my journey from suffering, emotionally and physically, to the inner assurance that I am a glorious spiritual being in the self-realization process, is meant to strengthen you as you go forward in your own journey.

May you find everything you need for today, here and now!

Chapter 1
My Beginning

I survived. I was the only one. It wasn't anything I had done. I was only two and a half. My dad saved my life. I screamed, standing in my crib in my mom and dad's bedroom. My throat burned, my face burned. He carried me outside and laid me down on the lawn in front of our house.

I have told the story too many times. The details pieced together from what relatives told me are a bit hazy now so many decades have passed. Someone said my dad threw me out the front window and I was found on the lawn, but isn't it more likely the window blew out when the furnace exploded? So I do not know for sure what happened only that he saved me from dying in that burning house.

He died in the hospital soon after from burns (and maybe from the smoke) because he kept going back into the house to try to rescue my two older sisters, Susie and Peggy. They died in the house. Their bedroom was at the back, beyond the kitchen. No one could get past the flames to get them out. One of the girls was found praying beside her bed. The other was found in the hallway. It was April, 1958.

Mom and I were the only ones in our family of five who survived. The difference between our experiences was that I had been in the house and I now had third-degree burns on my arms, legs, chest and face. Mom had been at Grandma's house putting a box of meat from her brother, Uncle Bill, the butcher, into Grandma's freezer. Grandma and Grandpa owned most of the block. Their house was up the street, two doors from ours. Mom and Grandma didn't know our house was on fire until the fire trucks came and they went out to the street to see what was going on. I can only imagine how traumatic that was.

I suspect I lived in the hospital for several months after that. A few years ago, I asked my Great Uncle Dan how long I was in the hospital. He couldn't remember, too many decades past. Now all those family members who were around back then are gone. Too much time has passed to get answers.

I have vague memories of an unfamiliar place, sitting in a crib, looking out the windows, loneliness and tears. Because of the cold floors and the empty room, I guess it was the hospital. I don't remember the pain, just a peculiar, black, lacy substance on some of my skin that would peel away.

The truth is I didn't figure out the bit about the lacy black skin for decades. I always had an unusual attraction to objects that had lots of holes, like a dead saguaro cactus, or any object with deep, small round holes. Once I realized this, black, holey, lacy things were even more intriguing to me. Eventually the pieces began to fit together and I understood. Now, I believe it was the black, dead skin that had to be peeled away daily as my burns healed that created such a strange fascination for me. I still don't remember the pain.

So I survived and life went on. My mom, who wasn't in the fire, but had lost her husband and two daughters, went to work as a bookkeeper in the lumber industry. I can't tell you how she was affected by her losses. She didn't talk about it. She said she tried to talk to a minister, but it didn't help her understand how God could let her children die.

I wish I remembered how old I was when she told me how she felt after the fire had wiped out her life. I guess I was four, but why would a parent say these things to a four-year-old?

She told me she wanted to commit suicide and actually thought it through one day while sitting in the bathtub at Grandma's house, holding the razor. She said she decided not to kill herself because she wanted to see how everything turned out, to see what would happen next. Such a simple answer. Her decision had nothing to do with me. She wanted to see what would happen next. It jarred me to the core. What she said has hurt all of my life.

I have talked about what she told me with several people, hoping it would help me not to feel so unwanted, that it might take away the ache. Possibly, because she told me her reason for not giving up, I always believed she would have been happier if my dad and sisters had lived and I had died instead. I understood her pain and loss better when she told me she felt suicidal, but then I felt so unimportant to her. I wasn't enough of a reason for her to live. She told me this herself.

After the fire, I stayed with Grandma a lot. Mom went to work. Grandma made me feel good. She may have lost her son, but she never said anything to me about it.

Grandma rubbed my arm down with lotion several times a day. It itched horribly all the time. I really wanted to scratch, but Mom and Grandma wouldn't let me. They taught me to rub the burns with the palm of my hand. I would even rub my arm vigorously when they weren't watching. I was happy to not scratch at it, just so long as I could do something to stop the terrible itching.

As far as I remember, I always had complete use of my arm. Grandma told me it was thanks to the nurses. Not through physical therapy (did that even exist then?), but because the nurses played ball with me and I played with them. Enough of the tissue grew back, connected and worked correctly that although both of my arms appear to me slightly unusual in shape, and definitely scarred, they work beautifully for baseball, typing, driving, and living. I am so very grateful.

I remember a day when Grandma rubbed lotion into my arm while we sat on the couch in her living room. She told me my arm made me special, because, "We can never ever lose you. You are the only little girl in the world who has an arm just like this." She explained, she and my mom could always find me and recognize me. I felt delighted and astonished. I cherish that moment and her. She made me feel loved and important over and over until I became an adult.

I have never been self-conscious about my arm. I don't cover it with long sleeves. I was teased by kids when I was in school. I'll never forget one boy's comments when we were in fifth grade. He called me "a burnt pig." What a shocker! It was the worst thing a kid had ever said to me. At the same time, I think what bothered me most was that he called me a pig. My surprise was due to my thinking there was nothing wrong with having burns. I suspected he thought I was fat, but how could my burns be used in an epithet?

As a teacher, I faced it too but the students were kinder. One of my first years of teaching, a middle school boy said I looked like Wonder Woman, but they had made a mistake when building my bionic arm. That struck me as pretty funny.

After the fire, my mom couldn't be there for me; she was grieving and surviving. She drank more and more. I didn't get what I wanted from her (love and attention). The cuddling I wanted wasn't possible because the front of my body was badly burned. When I was in my early twenties, she said she liked that I always hugged her hello and goodbye; she didn't know where I learned it because she has never been like that. So, cuddling and hugs I craved, probably because I went without.

Today I recognize a gift in the loneliness I developed in those experiences. My mom unknowingly, in her own pain, gifted me a desire – a deep yearning for more: more love, more comfort, more time and more attention. Always yearning for more drove me to seek: to seek something to help me. Originally, I thought it was in another person. I thought my mom had what I wanted and needed. Later, I'd want others to help me, even to fix me. I thought others had what I wanted. Eventually I realized my need for love and comfort were only marginally met by people so I transferred all that to a deep desire for God. That yearning must be why the song *Breathe* sung by Kathryn Scott spoke to me when I heard it. I related to her hunger and desperation for that essence we call God.

I believe on a karmic level it served me to be the burnt baby for all those months, when my pain was so great and the burns so deep, that people couldn't touch the front of me for a long while. I felt very lonely. The loneliness was also created by what felt like long periods sitting in my crib in the hospital, wondering where my family went and why they weren't there with me. I think my Grandmother visited me. I remember blue angels visiting, talking with me at night. I liked them. But mostly I remember sitting in a cold, empty place looking out the windows wondering what had happened.

The newspaper clipping is from the newspaper in the town I lived in at the time of the fire: April, 1958. It shows the devastation that changed my mother's, my grandmother's and my life.

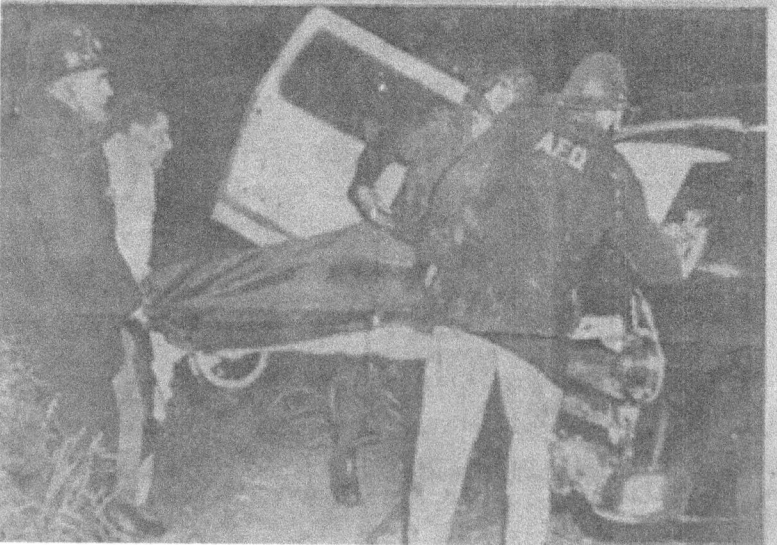

Chapter 2
The Law of Cause and Effect

I said earlier the losses, the emptiness and loneliness, created a deep yearning for love. My early twenties were spent looking for love in all the wrong places, which never satisfied my emotional needs. There were some wonderful men in my life during that time, but that surely wasn't the whole of my experience.

So much had happened in my life. I lost my dad and sisters, as I explained, at age two and a half; and later my stepdad when I was nine; and my mom was killed when I was twenty-five. Still, I have come to live in hope, faith and trust.

There were moments that felt hopeless. They eventually passed. There are answers. There is meaning. There is direction.

This is possible because we are continuous, forever, infinite beings. We all are. We always have been and always will exist. (Well, there was that initial separation from the Totality of All That Is, and there will be the eventual unification with all into oneness. Let's save that discussion for a later date).

Because of the fire, and the unhappiness I lived with and saw in my family members, I was compelled to find answers. I searched for what I needed to know. I began the seeking phase of my life in my teens.

I needed to know about alcoholism. And of course, once I heard the term "survivor's guilt," I had to understand that also.

I researched depression. From all this reading and asking questions of therapists, I got an inkling of what was going on. I learned about Adult Children of Alcoholics (and dysfunctional families) and said, "Aha, of course, that's me!" I came to understand more about where I came from. Based on observations of people around me, I knew that their religions hadn't helped them enough; they were grieving, drinking and unhappy. My mom had told me how she never understood how God could take her children when other children were unwanted. I set out to get more answers.

I read psychology and self-help books, beginning at age fourteen. Later, I joined a Buddhist sect when I was seventeen. That was where and when I learned about the Law of Cause and Effect and I realized there were actually always reasons why bad things happened.

I wanted to know why my life had been this way, and why so much pain too. I learned that cause and effect was more than what people generally referred to as karma. It is that in each and every decision made, each and every choice creates the patterns in our lives. We can change it in a moment. We can keep on the same trajectory for life times.

It is easy to see in a card game. When I play spider solitaire on the computer, I can see each card choice causing a different outcome. If I put the card on one pile, something happens; if I put it into a different pile, then something else happens. One choice will make the game flow. Another choice can stop all progress in the game.

So it is with all of life. Each decision an animal makes in a moment determines if it has a longer or a shorter life. Each decision you and I make creates an outcome.

When I taught school, we called this phenomenon 'choices and consequences': every choice, every action has a consequence. I'd explain to my students: Be sure your choices are something you really want and that you can live with the consequences – because that's just how it works.

When students did their homework and brought it to school the next day, everything related to turning in homework that day went smoothly. That is cause and effect. Of course, many students experienced the opposite – they forgot their homework and had to live with the unpleasant consequences.

When a student let his anger out at a bully on the basketball court and said all the things that were pent up inside, swore and threatened, that was a cause and there were consequences. That's the effect. Whether the consequence is a school staff person intervening or the bully kicking his butt later, it is a consequence (result). It's all because of the cause – the thing he did – that triggered it. What the bully experienced was the effect of his earlier actions (causes). It goes on and on. There was a cause that made the bully angry and mean in the first place.

The implication of cause and effect, of decisions and actions, of all the intricate interplay through lifetimes is too complex to full comprehend for most of us. The glimpse of understanding how and why we have created our lives in particular ways might be overwhelming while still fascinating and worthy of contemplation.

Chapter 3
We Create Our Life

O ur time here in these bodies that obscure our light, feels dense and at the same time it represents the consolidation of everything we've been, everything we learned and experienced (all cause and effect), and characterizes everything we want for our current experience.

I explained the Law of Cause and Effect to my Aunt Barbara and Uncle Lee back in the late '70s. I upset her when I said just as we've created our lives; our bodies are our creations too. Due to polio when she was young, her hips, legs and ankles were painfully affected. She didn't say a word to me, but after that conversation, she researched Buddhist teachings. My Uncle Lee told me later that she was okay with it. She accepted the concept of cause and effect. I wish I knew more about her thinking at the time. I wonder how it became okay for her.

It is hard to understand why anyone would choose a life with any debilitating disease or disorder, but obviously we do. Why would one choose that kind of body and that kind of experience? You might object like Aunt Barbara, or you might say I created this body intentionally? Or if without a disease or disorder, you might think this body may have its nice parts, but why would I make it so round – or what about the receding hairline, or the large ears, or the thick ankles? And I suggest:

Go deeper and reveal to yourself why. You had a purpose in it. It is a matter of bringing it to a conscious level. Every speck on our skin was created for a reason. Each relative we chose to play a part in this life speaks of who and what we've chosen to experience. Recognizing our responsibility in the lives we've created isn't blaming. Taking responsibility for creating ourselves in each specific way with the beauty, the perfection and the challenges remains the task to master.

The character traits we bring in with us serve us well, too. I love the determination and drive that are naturally mine. Granted, the drive part gets old at times. The determination has empowered me to achieve in school and work. It is getting this book written. I imagine I have these well-developed traits because they make it possible to fulfill my purpose in this life.

Our karma, when seen in its simplest form, is easiest to understand: just action and consequence. When we look at our lives and want to understand our karma, it takes seeing the context, the history, and the people involved to figure it out. It appears too complicated.

A small incident that made me unhappy helped me to see karma a bit clearer upon reflection. My husband and I had returned from a trip to Paris. As I put the new *café au lait* cups we had purchased into the cupboard, I chipped one. That upset me a lot. I wondered why I had done such a thing. Then I noticed how similar this annoyance was to the annoyance I'd felt when I saw my husband looking uncomfortable in a social situation in a museum café outside Paris. His vulnerability in that setting bothered me deeply. I was afraid. It wasn't a place or time that I could journal or meditate in order to understand why the situation brought up fear. Surprisingly, the incident with the chipped cup brought it all right back to me. I was unhappy because he showed vulnerability. His vulnerability scared me and I didn't deal with it. Now, in the safety of my home, without the challenges of travel in a country where I don't speak their language; plus with the resources of a few trusted, wise people, I could go deeper and see that the chipped cup (effect) was due to my fear, my discomfort that was unresolved (cause). From all that, I learned I needed to address my ability to be okay with my husband's vulnerability, that I needed to look at my fear and where it was coming from, and what I could do for myself to feel more secure and safe. All that arose from an incident in a café and a chipped cup a week later. Nice.

Considering our lives, the many people involved and the many actions (causes) over time, then understanding our karma is a complex challenge. It isn't simple. I can't overstate the importance of comprehending the patterns and meditating on each question. My dreams brought some understanding of the purpose of some of the events in my life. The process of coming to understand why the particular events occurred in my life has taken decades of perseverance.

This might help. Author Dorena Rode explains more in her blog. Check it out at: http://tesli.org/blog/karma/

Four Characteristics of Karma

- All actions lead to a result of similar type.
- The consequences are greater than the original action.
- If you experience something, you must have done the causal action in the past.
- Once you do the action, the result cannot be lost.

This understanding creates a desire in me to continue living in awareness of my actions and thoughts. I want peace and joy in my life. If I carefully choose how I act in the world, then I create a happier, easier life.

When I don't choose well, it's pretty painful. Once, while entering Costco, I spoke rudely to the young man checking for Costco cards at the door. The whole time I was in the store I repeated to myself what I had said to him. I played it over and over in my head and felt like crap. On the way out of the store, I apologized to him. That humiliating event truly impacted how I treat store employees ever since that day. My discomfort with myself motivated me to never humiliate myself that way again. I changed the karma I created in that negative statement when entering the store by taking responsibility, by apologizing, by using the next moment to change my future behaviors – thus creating less-unpleasant karma coming back to me.

Examining our lives using a paradigm that makes sense, like the Law of Cause and Effect, changed everything for me. It means that I, or we, create opportunity with every decision. Every action can create a different, healthier future. As much as it makes me responsible for my life, it empowers me to realize that I can create the life I want.

Chapter 4
Multiple Lives

What came before this life? If I assert I am a continuous and forever being, then there must be more than this life. Who was I, and what did I do, before I came into this life? It appears this life was created by all I did before, and by what I intend to accomplish this time around. The concept of reincarnation always made sense to me. To create a soul for such a brief period of time (to live for days or to 90 years) seemed a waste of a soul. Plus, I learned along the way that some sects of Buddhism teach reincarnation. For example, when selecting a Dalai Lama, the lamas look for a particular reincarnated being. That child often has memory of who he was before. The selection process is a major undertaking, with an expectation that there is a particular person who has done the job before and will do it again.

The familiarity we feel with objects, people and places also provides evidence. When I was about fifteen and riding in a car through Nevada, I had a moment when – although I'd never been on that particular highway – I knew with certainty there was a lake around the next bend. It was the first time I remember having awareness, then getting validation of its accuracy immediately afterward.

Later, when I read books, many of them told about things I was certain I had experienced (for instance, what the Egyptian student went through in the book *Initiation*). Once, in meditation, I observed myself sitting in a cave with a group of children, waiting for Jesus to arrive. When he did, and I looked into his eyes, I was overwhelmed by total unconditional love. The love and the joy it brought have always remained with me when I think about him or replay that moment in my mind.

In other meditations, I remembered sacrifice – including the sacrifice of my own life in a Roman amphitheater – even walking in the underground hallways to the arena, knowing full well that animals would soon tear me and the others apart. I carried myself with the conviction that it was better to die that way than to recant my beliefs because the ruling party demanded complete allegiance.

These appear to be past-life memories. I can't tell you how many lives I've had, although I've come to accept that it is more than I thought possible. The memories come in dreams, in meditations and sometimes just in recognition of a place. Once the memories came while walking in Venice, Italy. I came into the piazza in front of St. Mark's Basilica. When I turned and saw the building for the first time, tears welled up in my eyes and I felt immediately drawn to it. Once inside the Basilica, I kept hearing (inside my head), "This is for you." I still don't know exactly what it meant. I do know that I felt joy being there. I am not Catholic, but the place held deep, special meaning for me.

Another memory came when I met my friend Betty's dog, Sunny. How I loved that dog. I am not a "dog person." But when I was with Sunny, I'd lie on the floor and cuddle and pet him and simply be happy. I could see in my mind's eye a time when we romped in fields enjoying the sunshine. That doesn't resemble anything I am aware of in this life.

A common experience for lots of people is meeting someone for the first time and recognizing him or her, but not knowing why. When I met the woman who would become my

Reiki instructor, I knew I knew her, while at the same time I knew I'd never met her before – at least not in this life. Although I don't know her well, I've always been fond of her.

These mystical experiences aren't unique to me. Evidence that we are continuous beings, only transitioning with death, occurred for my sister, Brenda, too. She said she realized Mom didn't die when she was killed because Mom visited her the day after the shooting. Mom gave her reassurance and love. Brenda discovered that Mom continued beyond death. My paternal grandmother said she heard her husband talking to her in their bedroom soon after his death. Aunt Jan said she had died while undergoing surgery and viewed the revival of her body from a point near the ceiling of the operating room. She also said her mother and others (all deceased) greeted her and invited her to come to the light with them. She declined, explaining she had unfinished business on Earth. She lived over twenty years after that.

So rather than going on with more stories, I'll sum it up, acknowledging that I live with certainty that all of us are infinite, continuous beings, coming into realization of our true selves. We always have been and always will be.

The ways we live our lives, the decisions we make, the conclusions we come to, our actions and intentions, all go together from each life to determine the next one. In these lives we often vow never to do something again, or we promise ourselves we will have certain things. We also choose to meet with many of the same people again and again for a variety of reasons: sometimes for unfinished business, sometimes for love, and sometimes for karma. We do this reincarnation thing to learn and to experience ourselves in as many ways as possible.

Chapter 5

Abuse

The suffering that I and millions of others have experienced can be healed and released. Whether our pain originated in childhood abuse, war, torture, verbal abuse, rape, emotional or physical neglect, the path to inner peace already exists. It was forged by others before us.

Today, I step more into the light and move beyond surviving. Yes, I am good at surviving. I explained it in Chapter One, and there is more as you continue to read.

I established a sense of success in my career and in relationships. Still, it felt as though something was missing and although I was successful, I suffered with depression. Especially as a teen, and in my early twenties, just the simplest things like getting out of bed or washing my hair felt like a burden, just too much. I was always tired and fearful.

We know many, many, many women have been abused; molested as girls, raped as young women. We know that women and men use weight as a coping mechanism, using their fat as a shield to say to the world: "Don't see me, don't hurt me." Their bodies, our bodies show our thinking, "I must protect myself. I'm only safe if I'm invisible. I'm afraid."

Healing and moving forward means we acknowledge and take responsibility for our lives, not for the abuse that was forced upon us. With an overweight body, we can acknowledge the cause: some kind of pain. There is always something that caused the emotional pain. Identifying it takes looking inward. Lacking a sense of safety, as I mentioned above, is just one reason for developing coping mechanisms. The reasons are unique to each person. More than once, I asked professionals to help me. More so now, I go within and ask for help and guidance. Nothing need remain stuck in the "I just don't know why I'm ..." thinking. Answers and change are possible. Inner peace is possible.

Most children never received counseling after being molested – neither boys nor girls. Families denied what happened. Some parents even blame the children. Children blame themselves. In adulthood, victims often continue to hold themselves responsible, when the truth is their safety and well-being as children were dependent on the adults in their lives being responsible. It usually takes professional help for people to free themselves from the residual guilt, shame and self-loathing.

Children kept the secrets, believing they couldn't trust people, fearing retribution and living with the shame. Thinking, if it is found out, what will happen? Frequently, perpetrators threaten their victims' lives and the lives of their loved ones to keep them silent. So the victims worry that the threats will be carried out. Few families are healthy enough to get professional help for the child, to allow other family members to know, to let school professionals know – and to protect their children.

Often those who couldn't protect their children had survived victimization themselves. They weren't protected as children. They most likely didn't get counseling. How can one know what to do if one hasn't been shown a better way?

Fortunately, today, we empower more children with awareness, teaching "stranger danger," and teaching that the areas covered by a bathing suit are private – and that no one touches these areas but the child or the parent. When abuse occurs, we encourage children to report it.

I worked with a man who, because of his drinking problem, was inappropriate with his young daughter one night. He and his wife had taught her to report if anyone ever touched her in the "bathing suit" areas. She did so immediately. That was the first and only time she had that experience with him. He paid a high price with his family and in his career for his behaviors. Hopefully, the girl was supported sufficiently through the experience to never undergo violation of her body again.

We have legal services and court systems today that are created solely to assist the abused child through the reporting process. When many of the people who were molested by priests and by coaches spoke out, it increased our society's awareness of molestation. That empowered others to speak up too.

We live in a world developing kindness for the wounded. There is progress to be made in the consciousness of many, but for now it is good to know we have improved our awareness and response – compared to the secretiveness, that we practiced in the past.

A sense of powerlessness stays with the victims and bleeds into many areas of their lives. Yes, it is painful to think of all that we have no control over: from considering whether my husband makes it safely home from work today, whether my mother-in-law is happy, whether my niece can ever have children. Even these thoughts can make me feel powerless and these are not monumental like the serious victimization I have discussed in this book.

That sense of victimization can be undone. I remember a male friend in college explaining to me the difference between women who walked with their heads down, and women who held their heads up and walked with a posture of empowerment. It dawned on me that I had walked with a big V (V for victim) on my forehead – and I could change that.

Right after college, I went through a period of consciously replaying my dreams with better endings. The nightmares where I wanted to run, but could hardly move my legs, began to change to the ability to run fast. The endless fearful attempts to cross railroad tracks safely in dreams eventually came to an end. That phase of growth culminated in a dream where a police officer was inappropriate with me – so I slugged him full on in the face. Talk about feeling empowered!

That sense of powerlessness, of being a victim, often results in compulsion and obsession. It might, for example, involve thinking, "I don't have any money. I guess I'll use my charge cards (to the limit)." Or thinking, "Oh, I've eaten too much, but at the next meal I'll eat less." Then, lo and behold, no follow-through – just another big meal, then feeling uncomfortable and guilty and perplexed. That is powerlessness.

There is a point where powerless ends. Recovery programs are great for this because the first step is to admit: "I am powerless over (name the substance or the behavior) and it makes my life unmanageable." That's good. Recognize the powerlessness. Then use strength greater than yours, whether it is your higher power or those people who are healthy and recovering in the program. Eventually we grow; we come to a place where we empower ourselves.

There is power to be had. It lies within us already. It comes from Source, Creator of All That Is and from our own divine spirit. That power is available to us as soon as we are ready. It comes in at some level and it usually is an incremental process.

It has taken me many years to come to peace with all that happened in the first twenty-five years of my life. All the tools and resources given here are what I used to create the lovely life I have now. I see all that has happened in my life differently than I used to. My spiritual seeking has guided me. I have made use of teachers, therapists, healers, books, my spiritual practice and programs to get to the more centered, peaceful way I am today.

Seeking, yes, I was desperately seeking: answers, help, some kind of inner peace – but that has changed. I don't have to look to others, although I do love a good class, a good book here and there. I have my own inner resources now. I can ask God directly. I can discern what voice is mine and what is God's.

All the work I've done has changed my perspective from blaming others for my unhappiness. I carried contempt and disgust at my perpetrators. Believe me, it has taken decades to release that, to recognize that I was a child and not responsible for any abuse that happened, no matter what the perpetrators told me. I did the work with therapists to gain a new perspective on those events. I did that work to find relief from guilt, victim thinking, and shame. One book that really opened my eyes about child sexual abuse, which also helped me focus on healing, was *Courage to Heal*. I highly recommend it and I also recommend seeing a therapist who is well trained in all aspects of childhood abuse.

Over the decades, I integrated my understanding of what happened to me (a house fire, molestations and rape) with my metaphysical studies and experiences. In adulthood, I came to peace with it gradually. The understanding and acceptance I carry now came incrementally, some of it in the last five years. The milder events were always firm in my memory. It is different with the repressed memories that have come to me in a variety of ways. They still arise. Now I notice them; then I integrate them with the other fragments of memory. It no longer traumatizes me. Instead, it's recognition of "Oh, there is more." In fact, there's a bit of gratitude for the new pieces of information, because the picture of the worst abuse is clearer.

Remembering it makes it easier to understand the ways it influenced my life.

Given the decades of work, today I even can say without malice, without shame, I think everything that has happened falls within the Law of Cause and Effect. The babysitter who molested me (within karmic teachings that's the effect) was female, because she was a representative to help me release karma from a past life. I have remembered parts of that life since I was in my teens. I atoned in this life for that life, for the many young women I had used whenever it suited me as a leader in a cult of women at that time. Those young women did my bidding. It was all about my pleasure. As far as I'm concerned, that was the cause of my babysitter's actions with me when she babysat me. For her, it may have been more about the molestations she underwent in her own childhood and this was just reenactment.

It is my understanding (gained through theta state meditation) that before I incarnated, I asked a different relative to please be the one who does sexual deeds with me when I am young (age six). I told him my soul needs and wants this kind of experience. Through it, I will release karma. I will use it to deepen myself. I will use it to help others. He wasn't sure he wanted to. He loves me, though, and agreed. This conversation took place before my birth. So I was the cause. I don't know his karma in it. Molestation was the effect that served me. Although they were confusing and shaming experiences, through them I released karma and deepened my compassion.

Blaming isn't necessary anymore. I am not a victim in my new understanding. Everything that has happened had a source and a purpose. I have done enough healing work and I have grown enough in spiritual awareness, that I am at peace with these events. At any time that shame or fear related to the abuse comes up for me, I do the work again to release it and be at peace again.

Maybe it would help to clarify that karma is cumulative. Grace is an intermediary I haven't discussed here. It's such a huge topic; still, Grace, however it comes, brings peace, too.

If you have been victimized in any way, please be assured that I in no way believe you are responsible for the molestations or abuse that occurred, nor are young men or women responsible for rapes they've undergone. The responsibility always belongs with the perpetrator. Coming to terms with abuse, torture or trauma is unique to each individual. In my case, I believe karma was behind all the events. For others it could be different. Take, for instance, the man who killed my mom. I don't know why he was the one to do it. I do believe my mom had a karmatic requirement to die in a tragedy like that and that there was purpose for my family (especially for my stepdad, Brenda, Mom and me) in that experience. So apparently someone needed to do it. Did the man who shot her do it because they had had a similar encounter in another life that required balancing? Or did it serve him in another way to kill and serve a long prison sentence? I don't know, but I am certain that nothing in all of that was accidental.

Chapter 6
Oneness

When we notice the similarities between others and ourselves, we open the door to love and to unity. When we see the similarities in our religions, whether Catholic or New Age or Jewish or any other, we open the door to communication, to trust and to peace.

In the book *Living Buddha, Living Christ* by Thich Nhat Hanh, he discusses the similarities of Christ and Buddha that show us the greatness that we each can aspire to. Although a Buddhist, he explains that he considers Jesus a spiritual ancestor and why he feels that way.

Books on similarity and unity of religions are beneficial. Recognizing the point is not to malign Christ, but to show the traits in the greatest teachers, in the paths that lead to service to humanity and even to self-realization. Studying their lives, studying their positive attributes can make a difference for us now. Full awareness and self-realization are attainable in this life.

I see beauty and godliness in every one of my clients and students that they have yet to recognize. Maybe it has been covered with years/decades/lifetimes of beliefs, experiences, trauma, and disbelief, but I tell you it is true. I just know that whenever I work with people in counseling, ThetaHealing®, or meditation classes, I see and feel the beauty in them while often they can't imagine themselves that way – so I help them move to self-acceptance and self-love.

The woundedness, the I-am-not-enough belief, affected everything in their lives. When they come to me as a student or a client I believe another part of them propels them toward healing. Maybe that's grace. Eventually all the dross can be released and the beautiful true self emerges. I stress this because I see it in others and I know it was true for me too. There is such peace for me today, but for a long time I lived with just the hope that my experience would improve, and that the periods of deep unhappiness would resolve.

Now I do what it takes to stay clear, open and peaceful. I trust that as oneness with others develops in me it develops in others too.

Chapter 7
Death Again

When I was four, my mom remarried. Clay was a tall, thin German-American with short hair and a mustache. I wore a stiff yellow dress and shiny black shoes as the flower girl in their wedding. I still have the picture of the three of us, posing for the camera. We moved to Washington State that year. This was my third new home in my short lifetime. Next, we moved to Eureka in Northern California and I started kindergarten. This is when I remember the serious arguments starting between Clay and Mom.

I entered kindergarten in Eureka after school had started. I don't know why. The teacher told us to get our crayons out of our desks, but my desk had no crayons. I didn't say a word then. I cried instead. It was a rough first day.

That year, I discovered white sugar and butter on white bread. Yummy. I suspect that was the beginning of the eating disorder I developed. I learned the poor kids down the street in the big, unfinished house could have as much sugar as they wanted on their cereal. That just seemed like heaven to me. I tried it too at home, but I got in trouble.

For the last six weeks of that school year, Mom and I moved to Santa Rosa to live with her favorite brother, Uncle Bill and his children. Their mom had left for a while. My stepdad stayed in Eureka. I went to kindergarten with my favorite cousin, who was my age. It was fun. She had two brothers. I really enjoyed having my cousins to play with all the time. Then Mom and I returned home.

Altogether, that made the third kindergarten I went to that year. I don't know why or how it is that I went to the one by my great-aunt's house, unless it was because she was babysitting me. However, I remember discussing the Three Stooges with the other students during naptime there.

I don't remember first grade. I attended school, but without looking it up, I cannot say where. I suspect the missing memories show a disconnect due to the sexual abuse perpetrated by a relative around that time.

When I was in second grade, my mom was pregnant. We had a stout little bulldog that snorted and drooled. He made Mom sick a lot. We moved again, this time back to Arcata, where I had been born, the next town up the coast from Eureka in California. We had a house right by Arcata High School. I remember a lot of details from this time period, such as asking to have my room painted purple, learning I loved raw oatmeal with sugar, also nightmares and a small fire.

When I was seven, in June of 1962, my little sister was born. Grandma called the school and had me come to the office so she could tell me on the phone. It felt odd to get special attention, and at the same time, warm and fuzzy. My little sister was tiny and dear. I loved to help take care of her, change her diaper, and give her a bottle. She made little gurgling, slurping sounds as she drank her bottle. I could hear her breathe through her tiny nose, too. I discovered that this is what love feels like!

To this day, I love her deeply. I know of no other person as precious to me as she is. We're seven years apart, and for that and many other reasons when we were young, I provided her with a lot of parenting. This still causes protective parental feelings in me for her now.

She lives thousands of miles away, in Minnesota, but we talk on the telephone almost every week, email each other frequently and see each other at least once a year. I am very proud of her. She put herself through college and became a legal secretary and bookkeeper. Now she is director for her county's Emergency Management Department and she volunteers as an EMT for the county ambulance service. Cool, huh?

Now back to the past: I remember two distinct nightmares when I was seven. One was that a fire was moving across the fields, coming toward my house. I could see it from my bedroom window and felt terrified and helpless.

The other dream was that a doctor brought my mom out of his office, after he had drained all the blood out of her. He handed her to me. She was dying. I put her in the car and wondered where I could take her to get her more blood. Where and how to get her fixed? Another cousin was with me in the car. I could drive. I asked him to hold her while I drove. I was desperate to save my mom, yet so unsure what I could do.

This was my first indication that something was wrong at home. Something was killing my mom, and I wanted to save her. Was the deep, deep sadness I saw in her because everyone she loved died in the fire? I didn't consciously realize she had a problem with alcohol until I was about eighteen; I did not consider that it was alcoholism until she died when she was forty-nine. She died so young. I was twenty-five. My sister was eighteen.

A peculiar thing happened while we lived in the little house on the hill by the high school in Arcata. One morning, the fireplace began to smolder, although we hadn't had a fire in it for days. Mom moved herself, my new baby sister and me out to my great-aunt's house. Clay wouldn't leave. He thought she was overreacting. I listened in amazement because even with as

31

young as I was I understood her fear and actions. The firemen came and put out the burning boards under the fireplace. I guess it was faulty construction; boards under bricks in a fireplace that eventually were exposed once the bricks aged, cracked and moved. My bird had been placed outside in his cage while the house filled with smoke. He escaped. I never saw him again. We moved immediately.

This move took us to a two-story farmhouse next to the coastal mountains. There were cows in the front pasture, fields all around, and a creek flowing behind the house. Mom planted a garden and Clay started to build a boat.

I joined Bluebirds, sold cookies and earned badges so I could go to summer camp. My cousin and I fished in the creek until the day I realized I didn't know how to fish – because I caught the fishhook in my thigh while casting.

I didn't know until I wrote this why I cried when I saw Clay running across the fields to come get me and carry me home. I wasn't in any pain. My cousin and I had laughed when we traced the fishing line and missing hook to my thigh. Yet, when I saw help was on its way, I began to cry. I think it was one of those moments of seeing someone, a dad, running to help me, to be there for me. I guess for just a moment there I had a dad who cared. Hmm, it still makes me tear up.

Mom and Clay's arguing worsened. Some of the arguments were about her staying out late after bowling on Tuesday nights. Apparently, she would go drinking with her friends. Back when I was five or six, she confided in me that he threatened to kill her. It happened at her mother's house. They had sent me outside while they argued. I don't know what the specific problem was that time. I remember she came outside and sat by me on the rickety wooden back steps. When she told me he wanted to kill her, I didn't know what to say. So I tried to comfort her and tell her it was against the law so he probably wouldn't. She said she didn't think he cared about the law.

This memory exhausts me. I know my mom often looked to me for comfort. This is the first evidence I remember of it. It was another part of the unhealthy role reversal we had, just like when she talked to me about not committing suicide when I was four or so. Being a child carrying a burden that is too heavy for even an adult to manage still makes me weary. I still remember clearly how bewildered I felt in those incomprehensible moments.

I guess Clay didn't drink much. I do have a picture of him on New Year's with a beer in his hand, and me on his lap wearing a sparkling party hat on my head. He had a handlebar moustache that was greased and twisted up so it curled. We were very cute.

Clay was killed in 1963 in a logging accident, working for one of my great-uncles, my real dad's uncle. Brenda was two. I was nine. Interesting isn't it that Brenda was the same age as me when she lost her dad.

There was no insurance money to help us manage. Mom went back to work. Clay's boat was never finished. It's funny how a little thing like that was highlighted in my mind. These losses caused me to believe you should do and say everything that is important with the people in your life that matter to you because you never know when they will be gone.

I had trouble accepting his death. I was in third grade. My dear and very caring (Great-) Uncle Dan picked me up from school one day and drove me home. I wondered why, because although I liked playing baseball with him and his son, this event was totally out of the ordinary. He was usually working in the woods until dark.

I waited for an explanation while he talked to me. He took me to another cousin's house nearby. As we drove up the long country driveway, he explained about the logging accident and the big fallen tree that wouldn't budge. Clay had been working on it. As he put a choker chain under it, the tree rolled and crushed him. Now, I don't know if that's what Uncle Dan said then or if I heard it later, because a few days after that, I discovered I was confused about the accident. I had changed the ending of what Dan said to be what I needed to hear.

We stayed with Uncle Dan's family for a while after that. I stopped my mom in the hallway of their house to ask when we would go visit Clay in the hospital. She said we wouldn't because he wasn't in the hospital. He was dead. It was a startling statement. She didn't touch me. I wondered how I could have been so wrong about what had happened.

Then she made me go to the family viewing services the night before his funeral. She told me later that she hadn't intended to, but decided I needed to see him so I would accept the fact that he was dead.

It was a horribly shocking experience. It still makes me cry. I remember looking in the casket and not recognizing his face or clothes, just his hands and his body. Clay had never worn a suit. I thought the worker guy that stood by the casket was who he looked like now. I sat on the red couch in that gaudy, over-decorated yet bleak room and cried. The worker man said things. I wanted to scream at him. It was awful. Clay wasn't even my real dad, but I wanted him back.

I'm not sure how his death affected Mom, although after the funeral I overheard her say that she thought she was a jinx when it came to husbands, so she shouldn't marry again. I think she did spend more time with her friends.

I haven't lived in Arcata since I was in ninth grade; still, I remember the names of all the bars around the plaza. There was *Toby and Jack's, the Alibi, the Office* and a few blocks away was the *Arcata Bowl*. I would sit outside and wait in the car, or sometimes I got to go inside and have an orange soda. I especially liked the building with the black and white tiles on the front. It gave me something to focus on as I tried to ward off the boredom.

At other times, I would call the bars trying to find my mom. Funny, I can't remember when or why I would do that, since I was usually with babysitters or family when she was gone.

I suspect several of my relatives and their families were suffering also, because some of my aunts and uncles drank so much. They didn't come home some days. Sometimes, family members would send one of the men in the family to drag them out of the bars and bring them home.

After Clay died, we moved again. This time it was back into town, right next to the railroad tracks (you adjust to the noise) and on the "right side of the tracks." This appeared to be important because the Portuguese families lived on the other side. Of course, racism is and was everywhere and we all lived not far from poverty. This was my eighth home. I was nine.

Here is another piece of the puzzle. Let's go back a minute to the threats I referred to in Chapter Five. In my case, my relative said he'd hurt my mom if I reported what he was doing with me. But when my stepdad Clay ridiculed him for being a pervert and liking sexual activity with a child, well, tension grew between them. My mom had told my stepdad that she discovered that this relative was molesting me. Apparently my stepdad had words with this relative about what he'd done to me.

My stepdad did work for him briefly, until there was a logging accident. The experienced loggers say the accident was preventable. People couldn't figure out why the accident happened. Why did Clay hook up the chain the old-fashioned way, which was known to be dangerous? Why didn't he do it the correct way – the way loggers were doing things now?

Granted, my stepdad was inexperienced. But why didn't my relative watch out for him? Clay wasn't a logger. He was a diesel mechanic who worked on big rigs. He was just helping out. I would guess there was old karma between this relative and my stepdad that played out that day.

Almost every child who is molested is told that something horrifyingly worse will happen to them if they don't keep what is happening (the abuse) a secret. Threats silenced me for a long, long time too. I did not start remembering what that relative had done to me until I was in my thirties.

Chapter 8
Beyond Pain

As I grew up, I would sometimes hear my mom in the middle of the night sobbing while she sat by herself at the kitchen table. When I went out to the kitchen to comfort her a few times, and asked her what was wrong, she said it was because she lost her daughters and my dad and how hard it was to live with that. A few times she said she was crying because the anniversary of their deaths was near. It still makes me cry to remember and feel her grief, her losses, her suffering. She told me, "Just go back to bed. There is nothing you can do." I felt so powerless. It was true there wasn't anything I could do and I'd return to bed. As time went by, I might hear her, but I didn't get up.

There was a point at which I realized that my mother didn't have what she needed to get over her losses. It created in me a desire for answers. I needed to know what would help a person with such immense pain. Although she was Christian, and even would surrender all that to Jesus and feel better for a while, she remained deeply unhappy and continued to suffer until she died at age forty-nine. Her faith didn't bring her peace. I wanted to know what would. Where is the solace we seek?

On top of that, she also couldn't stop drinking. In fact, she never even tried. I didn't want that life. I rejected it and insisted I would drink normally. So, my mom was a teacher for me in that way. She showed me what I didn't want out of life.

I also searched for meaning, for answers, which I found when I discovered Buddhism.

Considering life through the eyes of the Law of Cause and Effect means that everything in my life, EVERY thing, is because of a choice I made at some point. Understanding how it works is tricky, because we may remember when or why we made the decisions, or not. Or, I may even just wonder why I would have decided that for myself!

I wanted answers to my questions. For instance, why would I have done something like bringing horribly traumatizing events into my life? What about all the horrible things that happen in the world, too? That's all about karma. Questioning leads to deeper understanding.

I wondered why I put myself though the house fire and was the only survivor. Why would I choose an alcoholic mother and stepfather (my second stepfather)? Why experience rape? Good questions.

I have answers now. I've shared in this book how my understanding grew while learning about karma, discovering my responsibility in creating my life, and experiencing growth. This isn't about blaming me. It is about a new level of understanding. As I searched, and asked why, and as I grew in my spiritual awareness, I came to see how I created my life, however atrocious. Everyone is the creator of their lives, and each trait, each experience, each person playing a role in it has purpose. Nothing is accidental. Some of the insights came through dreams and visions, in therapy and meditation and others from spiritual teachers' guidance.

There was a time I fought the concept that I felt always buffeted about by the winds of life. I had no control. Bad things just happened. There was no safety in the world. I lived in fear, anxiety and depression. The seeking of answers and a way out of the pain began because I couldn't stand the feeling of powerlessness that I lived with.

Studying Buddhism is a good example of how I jumped into a practice to get everything I could. At seventeen, I joined a Buddhist sect that chants parts of the Lotus Sutra. Most of the time though, we chanted four words from the Lotus Sutra which carry the heart of its message. We chanted, "Nom Myoho Renge Kyo." They taught us to set intention on what we wanted. They also taught that chanting is like prayer; I can't pray to change others; I can pray and chant to change myself. Buddhism's teachings gave me new understanding. Realizing that we go on and on: in each life we have experiences, we react, we act, and all of that creates the karma, the effects we are living today. By learning that, I realized some of the reasons why things are the way they are. I wasn't just victim to the cruelty of life. Everything happened for a reason. I can understand those reasons. I can influence my karma. I can add positive causes through praying, chanting, forgiving, giving service, donating, loving and random acts of kindness.

While I was still devoted to that sect, my cat, which I'd had since seventh grade, became seriously sick with a urinary tract infection. I took him to the vet. The vet said he would treat him, but to not be too hopeful and it would take four or more days. I chanted with focused intention for healing for my dear cat, Poopee, and I saw a miracle. The more focused our heart and desire and love into our chanting (all causes), the greater the likelihood of a positive result (effect). Things change every time. The next time I talked with the vet, he said to me, "I've never seen a cat heal so quickly from that disorder." That validation convinced me there is power in the chanting. My Buddhist teachers had told me that chanting could change anything and bring miracles. I saw it myself.

About 200 of us were kneeling and chanting together at a beautiful Buddhist temple, on a cliff overlooking the Pacific, in Daly City. I paused because I could hear what sounded like angels singing. I heard exquisitely beautiful music and singing, but saw no visible source. The chanting continued and I joined back in. I never forgot that inspirational moment of hearing the angelic realms while with Buddhists.

Let me clarify I am not pushing any one religion. The religious concepts discussed here, taught by different groups and called different names, aren't separate things. They are all connected to the same source. Humans just draw lines, use different words, call things by different names and confuse themselves. Unification – helping each other grasp the commonalities in all the spiritual teachings, all the religious paths – is the point for me. Oneness underlies everything. If I look at what the groups have in common, I find how much all the teachings point to the same truths, virtues, and oneness. Peace comes in shifting each other, all of us, into unification.

I found Buddhism, like Christianity, has numerous branches (schools), and it has a history of starting with a great teacher, as well as profound teachings which are handed down verbally, then eventually written into texts and taught. Buddhist and Christian spiritual teachings, monks and monasteries have spread around the world, so there are now Buddhist temples all over the United States, too. Also, as in Christianity, there are different branches with subtle differences in theory and practice. For me, this diverts from the real value of the teachings, it distorts the power of the teachings and it shows how easily humans are divided.

It is significant to me that world peace has been discussed throughout my lifetime, maybe kicking off in the 1960s. It tells me peace is possible and that I can help facilitate movement to peace for all by focusing on the commonalities within the many different religions.

So even today several decades after studying with Buddhists and living in a Buddhist chapter house, I still chant, though maybe not in their preferred ways – namely sitting in front of the gohonzon (a scroll inscribed with parts of the Lotus Sutra) in my budsadon (a decorated box that the scroll hangs in) – but rather, chanting whenever I feel like it, using a free moment to bring forward more life force, to cultivate good karma, to send out positive intentions into the universe. It comes very easily. It feels right. Soka Gakkai International (SGI) still teaches this path to enlightenment in all big cities.

Because I've been a seeker, with a deep need to know about the different religions, I studied the Kabbalah with a group of women a few years ago. A school psychologist I worked with invited me to join her in a newly forming study group, an opportunity to study, embrace and understand something foreign to me. I have many Jewish friends and knew so little about their way. Actually I still know so little. It doesn't matter. I respect their ways. I found Kabbalah very informative and viable. I'm glad to know a little about another path.

Maybe next I'll study Islam, especially Sufism which fascinates me. I know nothing about Islam, and I know it has concepts and teachings that already match the good in other religions. I want to understand.

The truth is all of this isn't about religion: it is about a spiritual path, seeing the validity in all paths, and knowing that the religion can help or hamper the path. The teachings in every religion are valuable. It is humanity that has bogged it down in dogma and rules. Loving and practicing the teachings that ring true is the key.

Chapter 9
Accepting Love

O ver and over, I have had to allow the grief to flow, to release. It overwhelmed and scared me as if it could be neverending. Once I figured out that few adults could help me with it, I'd ask, "Creator, send me peace. Show me a way." Did I just hold on to old emotional pain and regrets, or did they continue to come up because there was so much to grieve? I'm not sure.

Back in the early '80s in a Grants Pass, Oregon church during an altar call, I first received the Holy Spirit. Shortly after that, my minister recommended I read a book by Ruth Stafford Peale (Reverend Norman Peale's wife), called *The Adventure of Being a Wife.* That is where I learned that the Holy Spirit is also called the Comforter. Her book might be considered seriously old-fashioned today, but I gleaned what I needed from it and added the Holy Spirit as my go-to along with God and Christ.

Surprising to me, I found that not a lot of people outside of charismatic churches know much about the Holy Spirit. I wanted to know more, so I kept asking people about it. I interviewed a Catholic priest, but he really had no experience with the Holy Spirit and was unable to further my understanding.

As I learned about the Holy Spirit, I discovered the gifts of spirit. The Bible lists the gifts of the Holy Spirit. Sources vary, but there appears to be a consensus that the gifts are wisdom, knowledge, faith, healing, miracles, prophecy, discerning spirits, tongues and interpretation of tongues. It is odd to me that although these are in the Bible, and many people follow the Bible to the letter, they don't appear comfortable with the gifts of the Holy Spirit. Consequently, I don't talk with most people about how they show up in my life.

KC Miller, founder of the Southwest Institute of Healing Arts in Tempe, Arizona, shared what worked for her. She would call out, "Holy Spirit, come to me. Holy Spirit, I need you now. Come to me." I didn't know I had permission to ask for help at that level. Silly me. I love how it feels when the Holy Spirit comes to me. There is love and comfort and ecstasy. My problems fall away. I like the idea that there is a force greater than me, not dependent on a person, but an invisible comforter that comes whenever asked. What a gift.

Always focusing on knowing or finding God has guided my whole life. I took a class in the mid-'70s titled Search Within, which was my introduction to the light. We were taught to use it in meditation. The light is sometimes seen in pictures emanating from the sky, from saints, from Christ, maybe even from Tibetan masters of the Far East. Simply put: I want that.

When I first learned about the light, I visualized wrapping myself in light while in meditation. I practiced regularly, visualizing bringing light in through the crown of the head until it filled up my body and entered every cell. Then I continued pulling in so much light from that extraordinary, unending source that after it filled the body, it overflowed out the crown chakra until it surrounded me in a cocoon of light. Then I just sat and enjoyed the higher vibrations and sense of well-being.

Also, using the same process, I wrapped a bubble of light around my car for protection. My husband has done this for years now, too. We especially do this when we travel on long trips together. For about a decade, I put light around my house every night as I'd go to sleep. I still start each meditation by bringing light down into my body and raising my vibrations.

I discovered when I studied ThetaHealing®, created by Vianna Stibal, she said when connecting with Creator of All That Is in the theta brain wave state of meditation, to experience the iridescent pearly white light and bring that down into your body. I love it when someone else's teaching reinforces my experience and beliefs.

I also work with the light to help others. When my sister first moved to Minnesota not long after our mom died, I visualized sending her pink blankets of light to wrap her in, and praying that she feel loved. About seven years ago, I made a CD with a how-to-section and three guided meditations that walk you through how to do these things. It is available through my website.

Chapter 10
Embrace Change

C hange is inevitable in our lives. Buddha taught that our lack of acceptance of how things are causes suffering. I find although I enjoy change – new inventions, new tools, travels and adventures – I get unnerved when the change doesn't match what I expected. Embracing change with an attitude of acceptance makes my life easier. Sometimes I work at it.

One change in Americans I've seen personally is the change from when men never hugged. How long ago was that? The 1960s? Then Leo Buscaglia came along and created a new cultural norm that it was good to hug. Known in some circles as Dr. Love, he hugged men and women at his conferences and encouraged them to hug each other too. It took off from there. Everybody hugs these days. Okay, some guys on the football field just smack their chests against each other, but that's contact, too. My uncles hug their sons and the sons tell their sons they love them. It is a new world that way.

These changes give me hope, even at the bleakest times. Hope keeps me going. It tells me things will be okay when I think I've repeatedly failed. My thinking has switched now. Even when I'm unhappy with a result or I'm feeling challenged, part of me knows that this moment is perfect just as it is. When it seems otherwise, it is just an illusion.

Watching the film *What Dreams May Come* was powerful and pivotal for me. Some scenes in the film represented things I had read about in metaphysical materials, such as the Akashic Records. Other parts had images that stirred something in me that I had to investigate. The film illustrated for me the illusion that we live, and how easy it is to get stuck in one's thinking and grief. It magically illustrated abstract concepts so I could understand and internalize them.

Seeing *The Matrix,* which I still watch occasionally, gives me visual images of this illusion we live. I need to see it to grasp that this reality is actually illusion. The illusion exists to provide what I want to experience right now. Being reminded I am living in illusion takes some of the power and drama out of life for me.

Reading Richard Bach's books also helped me understand reality versus illusion in creating my own life. *One* (that's the title) explains Bach's thoughts on other aspects of himself, and what he might have learned on the many roads he never took.

Seeing the more recent films *Lucy* and *Interstellar* prompted me again to consider living in full potentiality as Lucy did, and to see the irrelevance of time and space as the retired astronaut showed us.

Chapter 11
Self Love

I can love my ex-husband. I can love my old boyfriend from college. I can love my husband. These are different kinds of love, but they are love. I can love the person begging on the street or sleeping on a bench. I can love every child I meet. I can even love people I don't especially like. I don't have to spend time with them; I just have to love them. If I don't see anything l love, I ask God to help me discover it. I know they are God. That spark of God is still there in them, so I love that. When it's hard, I go to that higher place I found in meditation, and I know I can love anything and anyone from there. I can accept all people and events from there.

But can I love myself? Can I love all of myself: love my body, my personality, my past, and my weaknesses? Can I treat myself with the same regard I give to people I deeply respect?

Self-love doesn't come naturally to me. Because of the burns, I wanted to be as far from my body as I could get. It was too painful. Because of that, and the sexual and physical abuse I also experienced, I didn't have a love for my body. My desire was to get out of it. For much of my life, I would rather have been dead. That's odd to say, but it was my truth. Life was suffering.

My family members couldn't model self-love or teach it; they didn't have it for themselves. How could they show me? Most people are just soldiering on. They're just making the best of it. That was what I was taught to do, but I rejected it. It left me in too much pain. I believed that life could be better.

In developing self-love, I compare it to how I would treat a child or well-loved pet. What would I do for them? The kitties get to eat on a regular schedule, so I should do that for me, too. They always have water in their bowl and I should always have a glass of water nearby. So I have to pay attention to myself, and ask, "Do I have the right foods (semi-vegetarian, gluten free, organic) in the house?" By providing what I need and having it on hand on a regular basis, I avoid going out and getting junk food or sweets on the spur of the moment.

It also means, for me, going to bed at a reasonable hour and taking melatonin or tryptophan to ensure I sleep well. Also, I stay away from the scale. I can trust my body to tell me – and my mind to listen – so I know how my health is and how stable my weight is. My spirit and body can work together to provide just what I need to eat, and how much to exercise and rest.

Truly, getting-out-of-my-own-way has challenged me for years. Living in awareness of what is for my highest and best and the willingness to follow through on it requires my focus now. Using ThetaHealing®, I identify the beliefs holding me back. Beliefs like, "I can't do this. I've tried and failed." Beliefs like, "If I'm heavy, men won't bother me." As I release the negative, I become clearer and more mindful.

I don't diet anymore. I eat intuitively to the best of my ability, and avoid my allergy foods and the foods that easily trigger overeating (like sourdough bread and butter, or popcorn with butter and salt). If diets worked, everyone in this country would be healthy, with an average-sized body. I have read my share of diet books, and tried many ridiculous and expensive programs to lose weight. Uh, it didn't work. Now I do it by staying attuned to my needs and checking where my wants come from. I wasn't taught how to tune into my body and know what it needs. My family members didn't have that for themselves. I studied what works for people and added it into my life.

Chapter 12
Changing Awareness

A t times I've thought, "I tried and tried, I did the work. Why still more work?" I think it is the density of living on Earth. I may be a spiritual being having a physical experience, but the muck and mire of choices, fears, beliefs, traditions, and historic patterns held me bound in suffering.

Today feels like a new time period, probably because it is, since it follows 2012. I see lots on the web about it being the time that everyone can wake up: wake up to our true self. Some call it awakening, others ascension, and still others enlightenment or self-realization.

Thank goodness, there are those who have gone before, who left trails to follow. I only have to ask for help, take the time to figure out what works, and let those changes into my life – and just as important, at the same time release what no longer serves me. I love the Internet. I can get up in the middle of the night and research anything I'm contemplating. No waiting for the library to open or to buy a book.

Just as the 1960s Age of Aquarius stuff really meant change for us, then so does this time period.

I talk a lot about woo-woo (metaphysical) things, and I'd like to think we are all getting more comfortable with the concepts. The world is changing. My favorite example is yoga, a spiritual practice that came to the U.S. and became a popular physical practice for many. And yet, it is still a spiritual practice for others, especially in India. So what once was considered weird is now available as a class at the YMCA. The world changed. It is changing always. That is obvious. There are changes on another level. A level we don't see. Some say a veil is lifting. It is not something I can explain; I can say, though, that I sense changes. Some of the evidence I do see is how intuitive most people are becoming.

Developing my own inner knowing has taken decades. Meditation surely helped. I check with myself on all important matters and ask what is my highest and best. Learning to recognize the difference between my inner voice, regular mental blabbing, and my guide's voice means I can trust the inner guidance I receive. My true self will only guide me in ways that help, in ways that are good for me – never rushing me or applying pressure. I heard that inner guidance/wisdom this morning when I was reminded I was over focusing on details – and to let it go, relax a little more.

I started noticing my intuition in my early teen years with the I-know-who-is-calling-when-the-phone-rings incidents. Then there was the stage where you hear the answer before the person says it. Then manifesting parking spaces everywhere I go. That was the beginning. Later it was "knowing" when to get in the car, when to stay home, when to turn left. And learning to check within myself and know what is right for me. If I am uncertain, I just pause, calm myself, go into the higher space of meditation, or raise my consciousness to theta state and ask again, check again. The next right step appears. Even if it's as simple as whether I pick up the laundry first or stop at the post office first. Living from intuition and inner guidance feels right and makes life flow beautifully.

I used to use self-help books, hundreds of them. Now I ask for and listen to my inner guidance – and don't need a whole book. I've found myself in the bookstore, reading one chapter out of a book and putting the book back on the shelf because I'd gotten what I needed. For example, with the book *How God Changes Your Brain* by Andrew Newberg, M.D., I set it aside for a long time because it didn't speak to me at first. When I picked it up again, I skipped several chapters and found the meat I was looking for in the middle. Perfect. I used to think I had to finish a book, and I still do finish most books – but now I let my inner guidance tell me what, when and how much of a book I need.

More now than self-help books, I like to read the few spiritual books that have the spiritual teachers' energy connected with them it. After reading Swami Rama's *Masters of the Himalayas,* I felt him in my meditations and talked with him in my sleep. That's a powerful book. Using my inner guidance to select books, I find the masters who perfectly match what I need next. All of this applies to selecting classes to take, too.

Chapter 13
Autobiography

I used the requirement of writing a dissertation for my doctorate as an opportunity to explore and gain understanding from my life's experiences. It is titled: *Stronger at the Broken Places: Heuristic Inquiry*. In 2001, it was republished by a German company under the title *Stronger at the Broken Place: Heuristic Inquiry Growing up in Chaos and the Journey from Suffering to Self-Actualization,* and is available through many different sources, such as Barnes and Noble and Amazon. Chapter Two is autobiographical. Some of chapter two is included in this book.

Stronger at the Broken Places was a scholarly work, meant to investigate why children from dysfunctional family systems can grow up and be healthy, happy and productive; whereas others follow in the family's footsteps and act out the family's pain with addiction and criminal behavior – and certainly with little love in their lives. Writing it led me through a powerful transition of my own. My autobiography tells my story from age two and a half, when I survived the house fire, to my mid-forties. In delving into it I grew, understood myself better, and was freed a little more from the past.

Actually, I'm convinced that telling your story is a magnificent way to understand yourself and the players in your drama; to see cause and effect and to discover how you got to the point where you are today. In telling (writing) my story of self and rereading it to identify the themes within it, I saw patterns, including confusion and loss. Through that analytical process I gained even more from the autobiographical process. I realized how truly confused I had been as a child and a young woman.

As I delved deep into my autobiography, I remembered that when I was in the hospital recovering after the house fire, I wondered where my mom was. I felt deeply confused and thought "Where did everyone go?" I wondered why I was alone in such a cold, empty place and who these people who came around me were. Fortunately, the doctors and nurses were deeply caring individuals who really wanted to help me, wanted me to live and did so much to save me. I am deeply grateful to them. My mother and grandmother were so devastated by their own losses (my dad and two sisters) that they didn't visit me much, and when they did, they couldn't hold me because of the burns down the front of my body.

Another theme, in addition to confusion, that became apparent from the writing is loneliness. I'm sure you can imagine how I came to feel so alone and abandoned. That deep sense of loneliness has taken a long time to release. The tools I mentioned in this book: prayer, meditation, ThetaHealing®, journaling and lots of actions brought the gradual healing, the release of the confusion and loneliness.

Writing this book, sharing my losses, brings up grief again to process at another level. Doing breath work and the heart song (see *Advanced ThetaHealing® – Harnessing the Power of All that Is*) in between writing sessions is causing me to release older gunk (pain). I will do all it takes until I am totally free.

Chapter 14
Healing

When studying Christianity from an evangelical teacher, I learned the laying-on-of-hands type of healing. Later, from a spiritual teacher and healer, Betty Toohey, who trained at the Berkeley Psychic Institute, I learned energy healing. From another healer, I picked up two levels of Reiki. Just a few years ago, a Buddhist teacher, Dorena Rode taught me ThetaHealing®. I knew healing was possible because of the experience with my cat when I was about twenty-one. I also had read about healing and believed.

Now, mostly using ThetaHealing®, I have healed many conditions for others and myself. But let me clarify: I don't do the healing; the Creator is in charge of that. I just go into a theta state meditation, pray, and witness the changes. I identify to the best of my ability what is needed and go to God. This is ThetaHealing®. It was created by Vianna Stibal. For more information on ThetaHealing®, go to www.ThetaHealing.com.

God does the healing. I assist. Teachers gave me the technique; while the belief, willingness, and compassion were already within me. God does all the real work. Crucial to the effectiveness, though, is whether or not the patient allows the healing.

Last year our cat, Chocolate, wouldn't allow the ThetaHealing® I thought he needed to make him healthy. He looked so miserable. I knew he was sick. The healing wasn't working. I couldn't get him to the vet because he fought me so much. His fear was too great. Finally I found that I could relieve some of his symptoms using Reiki. He'd feel better for a few days, then appear to feel sick again. Finally, I understood he didn't want God to heal him. He wanted to die. I had to respect that. I found a vet who makes house calls. He came to the house and examined Chocolate, and determined he was dehydrated and had feline HIV and that he wouldn't live long. So we let Chocolate go. I truly believe it was what the kitty wanted. He had had four good years with us. He had been a stray we took in, so in the end, all was perfect because we had given Chocolate a loving, caring home with lots of yummy food. He showed me he was done with this particular life experience. His purpose was fulfilled. It made me cry today when I wrote this. I'm not sure why, other than I miss his big, boisterous self.

I was glad to be part of his process, of taking him in, getting him to trust us. He loved being king of our house. The middle of the bed was his. If we called him, he'd run to us and then flop down near us with a thud (he was a big guy), so we could pet his beautiful black and white long hair and scratch under his chin. You can see the perfection in it. Not everyone wants a long life. My other kitties often live to eighteen and twenty, but not Chocolate. He taught me more about healing. When ThetaHealing® doesn't work it is because it doesn't suit the person (or the cat) to be healed. It isn't what they want in their heart of hearts.

Chapter 15
Surrender

Although surrender might be the perfect state for letting go, for relinquishing control – and is recommended in recovery programs, in Christianity and in Hinduism just to name a few – it was really tough for me to get it. I analyzed it. I asked about it. I listened to people talk about it. I found I could surrender the big things in life, the big decisions, but not my every moment. In surrender, I am teachable. God has access to me, and brings the growth and changes I've requested, and whatever is for my highest good even if I didn't know to ask for it. The trick is how to stay in surrender.

A small but important miracle for me came the time I went to see my young friend, Marti, at work. She wasn't there, so once I got into my car I practiced surrender by saying to God, "Where do you want me to go? I have two hours, what would you like me to do? I'm all yours." From there I went to Fashion Square Mall in Scottsdale and walked into the courtyard for lunch. To my surprise, there was Marti sitting at a table with her boyfriend. I got to chat with her for a moment and moved on. In my mind was a big "WOW – look at what happened." I made myself available, asked for direction, and got exactly what I wanted and hadn't even thought to ask for. She and I, twenty-five years later, have a wonderful friendship: deep and meaningful. That event was just one of many that kept moving us close to the same path, the same place.

While surrendering every aspect of my life, I want to live my life in conjunction with what Creator wants for me. I ask God for higher wisdom and guidance for all activities in my life. I align myself with Creator, which means to draw as close as I can. When I surrender and go with what is for my highest good, life just flows! It is much easier. I realize I am in the state of surrender because I sense at those times I am living with ease and grace.

When I moved to Oregon to become a teacher, I had already trained at University of Nevada, Reno and become certified. Next, I wanted an Oregon teaching certificate. The Oregon Department of Education didn't think the Nevada program was adequate; they had lists of additional classes I needed to take. I surrendered, recognizing this was something I couldn't change and took a position as a teacher's aide in the Title One program in the school district in the town l lived in, enrolled in the first required class and prayed.

To my amazement, within a few months, the Department of Education changed the law, now making reciprocity between Oregon and other states much easier to obtain. I ended up taking only two courses and I got my teaching certificate immediately. In less than six months after moving to Oregon, I had my first full-time teaching position and my own brand-new, just built classroom. We moved students into it in January. I was deeply happy and impressed that God had changed the world for me. It seemed so easy and it happened in no time at all.

Surrendering, letting go, and staying close to God isn't easy, but it does make it possible for me to get through the challenges in life. The shock of my mother's death stunned me, and yet it was an opportunity to practice trusting others, letting go, surrendering and letting God nurture me and accepting life as it is.

Chapter 16
Loss Again

W hen Mom and her third husband told me in March 1981 that they had bought a business, a neighborhood tavern, I was horrified. They were excited. I wanted to shout at them, "What? I cannot believe you would do such a stupid thing. Don't you know you have trouble with alcohol?" For decades, they had both had drinking problems, and now they had purchased a place where they could drink all day and night. With no reason for them to hold back, I saw it as the beginning of their end.

My nightmare came true just two months later, on May 23rd, 1981. I was twenty-five and in my first year of teaching my small elementary special-education class. The school secretary interrupted the class by calling over the intercom system. She said I had a telephone call in the office, would I come up for it. I wondered why they would want me to leave my classroom for a call, but I complied. I left my kids with the teacher's aide. On the way to the office, I felt panicked and started running. When I arrived at the office, the secretary told me to take the call in the principal's office. I had already started to cry. I knew something was terribly wrong.

Mom's closest brother, my Uncle Bill, was on the telephone. He let me know it was he, but then he couldn't speak. I asked him, "Are my parents dead?"

"No," he replied, "Just your mom." He gave me a few of the details. She'd been shot twice in a robbery of their business, the bar, late at night. Her husband, my second stepdad, had been shot twice also, and was in intensive care at Washoe Medical Hospital. I cannot explain the anguish I felt. At the same time, this seemed inevitable. This horrible life. The people I needed and loved kept dying.

He told me when he would arrive in Reno. We made plans to meet at my parents' house. He told me my sister had already been contacted.

After hanging up the telephone, I turned and found the principal in the doorway, looking at me with concern. The secretary was at her desk looking at me too. I said I had to leave and go home; my mother had been killed. They nodded, and said to go; they would arrange to cover for me at the school. (Even while editing this I feel like crying. So many years pass, and the shock, grief and pain still come back.)

Leaving the office, walking down the hall, I found myself somewhat hugging the wall as I went. I started crying again and slipped into the backroom of the library to compose myself. Then I continued down the next hallway to my classroom. As the kids and our aide stopped working and stared at me, I grabbed my purse and keys, told the aide my parents had been shot, and that I had to go. She could talk to the principal. He would work things out for the classroom.

I vaguely remember the drive home. I didn't know what to do with myself. My roommates weren't home. I called my chiropractor. He came to the telephone immediately and talked with me. The one sentence he said that I found comforting was from the Bible. Something about God knowing every sparrow in the sky and the number of hairs on our heads. My mother is of more value than many sparrows. God will take care of her. Nothing is too small for His attention. I felt a little better.

When my roommates came home, I asked them to sit down in the living room with me; I had to talk to them. The minister of this spiritual group I lived with said she would listen and started walking around doing things. Emphatically I repeated that I needed them to sit down while I told them what had happened. They did. I explained what Uncle Bill had told me and said I would be leaving for a while. My roommate who was my age, and from Reno, offered to come with me, saying something about my not being alone and offering to help with the driving. Reno was 350 miles from Grants Pass, Oregon, where we lived.

We talked for hours as we drove in my brand-new, dark-green, four-door little Isuzu. I remember trying to figure out if I saw any of this coming. I told her about the last time I had seen Mom, about a month before this. Mom had asked me to come into her bedroom. She opened her jewelry box and took out a little box, opened it, and handed me the wedding ring that my dad, Ray Cockrum, had given her. It was so tiny and ancient looking. She told me she wanted me to have it now. I didn't even know she still had it. I felt awed that it would ever be mine to keep. Then she told me she had recently given my sister, Brenda, the wedding ring that Clay, Brenda's father, had given her when they married. I was touched.

In addition to that event, I reflected on the fact that the last time I had seen Mom she barely said goodbye and did not leave the barstool in their new business to walk to my car with me. My stepdad walked me out to the car. I thought that was very odd. He and I had never been friends. As my roommate and I talked about these events, we decided there had been a few hints of what was coming.

A few days later in the house, while going through Mom's things, I found birthday presents for my sister and me already set aside. It was easy to know which piece of jewelry was for whom. Hers was a charm bracelet with a horse on it. Our birthdays were only days away. Also, Mom's boss at Zale's Jewelry told me there were Christmas presents, again jewelry, which she had put on layaway for us. Amazingly, she had provided us both with gifts for our birthday and Christmas that year. Did she have a sense that her life was about to end? It meant a lot when our birthdays and Christmas came, as if she was a little closer and had thought to provide for us. It made me feel loved.

Uncle Bill, my sister and I went to the funeral parlor to make the arrangements. I was glad he was there, helping to arrange things. I didn't know what we were supposed to do. I felt so numb, mostly as if I were just watching things go on around me and following when I thought I should. God, it was so awkward. Brenda and I decided to have Mom wear her pink dress, although she never wore dresses. We picked out her casket together. I remember thinking, "How do you decide? Should cost come into the decision?" Finally, we chose a shiny, wooden and brass one with pretty, silky fabric lining the inside.

Again, just as in those days, I feel nauseated as I think back on those moments. The emotions were overwhelming. It was hard to keep them under control. I didn't know how to act: tough and hardened, or like a scared little girl, or like a capable young woman. I tried the latter, mostly for Brenda's sake. She always looked up to me. I felt it was my responsibility to be strong for her, to let her feel that she could lean on me.

It was critical to me that the casket be left closed. I felt strongly that I did not want to see her. I had been through it with my stepfather and an older cousin and I did not believe I could do it again. It is too ghastly looking at dead people. I wanted to think of her as alive, laughing at a joke or smoking a cigarette, anything but dead and still, not looking like herself.

Still, with this amount of thinking, feeling and remembering, I feel almost as bad as I did in the year or so after her death. Knowing I would never see her again. I could never do things with her again, like shopping or seeing a movie. That is an odd thought, since we had never done those things together before. God, how I wanted her back! Other than my near-death experience in the fire, this is the most painful thing in my life.

We buried Mom with my sisters who had died in the house fire. Everyone agreed that that was where she should be buried, even my stepdad, although with his surgeries and slow recovery I don't know how aware he was. Uncle Bill told me when he was visiting my stepdad in intensive care, just after the shooting, Dean asked, "How is Vivian doing?" He had to explain she didn't make it.

My stepdad never recovered from the grief and guilt he felt. He was the one who, after being shot twice in the abdomen, called the police. I thought that was impressive. The sad thing is, he wanted to save her and couldn't. He tried, but couldn't. He didn't have a belief system that comforted him. I felt bad for him and how lost he was without Mom.

I remember how I used to get headaches from crying so hard about her death and how she died. The funeral was excruciatingly painful. The family had taken my sister and me to buy flowers for the service. They were very pretty; we thought we'd gotten Mom's favorites and that made me happy.

When my sister, the relatives and I arrived at the funeral parlor, we stood around outside the side door where the family viewing area was. It was awkward as we prepared to go in. It appeared no one wanted to open the door. Once again, I did not know what I was supposed to do, so I opened the door and led the way. I looked up, saw the casket was open, and thought briefly I was in the wrong place because hers was supposed to be closed. Then, I looked in and saw her. I groaned and cried out, "No, it was supposed to be closed. I wasn't supposed to see her," and rushed back out the door. Outside again, I gasped for breath and cried. I thought I was going to fall on the ground. I think someone held me up and talked to me. I tried to explain and sobbed. In the distance, I could hear my sister getting upset. I couldn't let myself be the cause of more grief for her, so I forced myself to pull it together and told her, "No, no. It's okay. I am all right."

Gradually we all calmed down, walked in and sat down. One of my aunts, I don't remember who, offered to sit by me. She held my hand. Breathing and staying calm was hard. The poem the minister read about women and mothers really captured the spirit of what I thought would be the right things to say about Mom. Eventually it ended. Everyone went out to Mom and Dean's house. Neighbors brought food. With lots of food and lots of family and friends, it was wonderful and horrible at the same time.

Each time I edit this portion, the sadness returns. I guess I have to accept that the pain of this kind of experience never leaves. It gets shorter, but it comes back every time I remember the pain the entire family felt, my stepdad too. At least I had God, and a few people I went to for comfort. He only had a few people to talk to; the rest of his feelings were drowned in whiskey.

I forgot to mention that I was told that Mom did not suffer. I wish I could remember who told me, probably my uncle. He said because one of the bullets went through her lung, she died immediately. I liked that. The thought of a person I loved lying on the ground, slowly dying, was too much to live with.

Nevertheless, later I had a long talk with God about it, because I wanted more reassurances that death was not just a scary, painful thing. Rather than explaining exactly how I came to understand and find peace about it, let me just say God showed me how death is a wonderful thing. It was like in the movie that came out much later, *Ghost*. Something like the light came, and there is an awareness of the presence of God (in the form that person is comfortable with) just the way George Burns told us in the movie, *Oh God*. When questioned, he explained he had chosen to appear in a form John Denver would accept.

Anyway, God led me to believe that death is an awesome, uplifting, however not-even-the-end, hard-to-fathom experience. Because of Mom's faith in Christ, I think she was not alone and maybe was quite happy in death. I felt much better.

I know Uncle Bill had a hard time with Mom's death. She was his closest sister. She had helped raise him. Years later, he cried at my wedding because he missed my mom so much. I guess avoiding his grief made him neglect to take care of the headstone for Mom's grave. She was buried in Arcata, just seven miles from where he lived, but he never made the arrangements to have her taken there; my lawyer did.

It was sixteen years before we got the headstone on her grave. By then, my stepdad had died too. So, it worked out well after all, I made it a combined one. Both sides of the family helped me pay for it. I put a lot of thought into what it would say. Brenda liked what I came up with. I hoped it would satisfy everyone. It was a beautiful rose quartz stone. The top line said their last name; their first names were below it, then the years of their births and deaths. The bottom line said, "Loved by": and gave our three last names.

By the way, the police in Florida picked up the man who killed Mom and shot Dean. They extradited him to Nevada, where he was found guilty and sentenced to two life terms. My stepdad's testimony was very helpful to the prosecutors. The killer tried at least once to get out on appeal and was not successful. He's a cold-blooded killer, and although I'm sure he is miserable in prison, for everyone's safety I hope he stays there until he dies. Because he is a human being I can feel love for him too; I just don't want him free to kill someone else and do to their family what he did to mine.

(This article shows when he was found guilty.)

Maresca guilty; sentencing today

8/26/86
Reno
Gazette
Journal

By Michael Phillis/Gazette-Journal

Joseph Maresca was found guilty Monday of murdering Vivian Grady during a 1981 robbery of the Air Base Inn bar near Stead.

Maresca, 50, was also found guilty of attempting to murder her husband, Dean, and robbing the couple.

After an eight-day trial, the jury of six men and six women deliberated about five hours before convicting Maresca. The same jury will return to Washoe District Court today to sentence him to life in prison without possibility of parole or life with possibility of parole.

Washoe District Judge Peter Breen will later sentence Maresca on the attempted murder conviction, which carries a possible one- to 20-year sentence, and two counts of robbery, each with a possible five to 15 additional years.

Because the jury also found Maresca used a deadly weapon in commission of all the crimes, every sentence he gets will automatically be doubled, including the sentence for murder.

Dean Grady called police at 3:30 a.m. on May 21, 1981, to report he and his wife had been shot in a holdup. Mrs. Grady, 49, was already dead from bullet wounds to the chest and back when police arrived.

Grady, shot through the stomach, told a paramedic that a new customer, a scotch-drinking Joe, shot him and his wife. Grady, then 52, recovered fully from the wound, but died last year of natural causes.

Bar customer Ron McDermott told sheriff's detectives the Joe he met that night was the only customer still in the bar when he left around 1 a.m. He said Joe told him that he had recently pawned a typewriter, fur cape and jewelry.

Checking pawn records, detectives came up with the name of Joe Maresca and an address of 74 Volcano St. in Stead. A search of the mobile home produced a box of .38-caliber bullets — the same caliber used in the shooting — and two plastic containers holding $111 in quarters and nickels.

After Maresca called home that afternoon and learned detectives were at the house and wanted to question him, he fled. He was arrested Jan. 31 of this year in West Palm Beach, Fla.

During closing arguments, Assistant District Attorney Ed Basl told the jury, "Dean Grady speaks to you from his grave and he tells you Joe shot him."

But defense attorney Michael Specchio pointed to the fact Grady had been drinking heavily the night he was shot and to inconsistent statements Grady made three weeks later in the hospital and after his release.

"The statements of Dean Grady are not mere contradictions based on confusion," Specchio said. "He flat out contradicted himself on many occasions on who shot him."

Grady said at different times that the one person who shot him fired with two guns — contradicted by ballistics evidence — at another time that two people did the shooting and every occasion after the night of the shooting that the killer drank tequila.

Basl said most of the inconsistencies came when Grady was in the hospital under heavy medication and had difficulty talking at all.

Basl called the testimony of an FBI expert matching the chemical composition of the bullets found in Maresca's mobile home and the five slugs recovered from the shooting a "direct and irrefutable link" to Maresca.

The FBI expert said the five slugs recovered from the shooting had to have either come from the same box as the 19

See MURDER, page 2C

69

Chapter 17
Making Decisions

W hat I was advised to do when uncertain about the best direction to take in my life was to ask three people their opinion on my planned course of action. I don't have to do what any of them says; I just want to get input and perspective.

That really helped me handle the panic I felt when, about three years ago, I learned Joseph Maresca, the man who had killed my mom in May, 1981, was released from prison before his term was up.

Maresca was convicted of the murder of my mother, attempted murder of my stepdad, and two counts of robbery with the use of a deadly weapon. He was sentenced to life without the possibility of parole, plus forty consecutive years and two concurrent thirty-year terms. For just the $350 he got in the robbery, he destroyed a family and ruined his own life. He then left the state, escaping to Florida until captured.

I discovered that even with a sentence like that, he was released a few years early, so the state could save money. Our family wasn't notified, as is legally required when parole is given and a prison term cut short. At the time of his release, he was about eighty years old. I was extremely hurt and angry, mostly because I had always wanted him locked up permanently as the sentencing had indicated. I didn't want him to kill anyone else. Murder appeared to come easily to him.

What stumped me about his release was how to tell my sister. I don't think she knew. I knew it would upset me to tell her and I didn't want to upset her, too.

So, following the "Don't make a decision when you are conflicted or uncertain what to do about something important to you. Check in with others for guidance and then do what feels best for you" advice, I contacted three friends who have drawn me to them because of their spirituality. After hearing their responses and suggestions, I decided to heal myself more so I wouldn't be in so much pain about it, and so I could tell my sister without adding my upset to the conversation.

Months later, it seemed the urgency to tell her passed and I never did. I intend to, though before she reads this book!

Anyway, the responses from my friends helped me to know I had to take care of myself first. (As they say on the airplanes, put the oxygen mask on yourself first; then attend to others.) Yep. I did that and the need to tell my sister about Maresca's early release fell away. I don't know if she had a need to know. We'll find out later (before this book comes out), when I do tell her.

My ability to get my own guidance has evolved. I do it myself now mostly. That inner knowing is such a Godsend. It was a while in coming. I always have the option of asking people I trust about important matters, if I choose. I'm grateful that I usually just slow down, check in, and surrender. Then the guidance I need comes from within me. I either hear it or just know.

Okay, so I sent an email to my sister about some of the things in the book, to be certain she could live with them being published. When I approached her about Maresca getting released, she said she already knew and didn't tell me because she didn't want to upset me. Ironic.

Chapter 18
Journeys

I left my parents at age seventeen to get married, so I could take a different path, to start out on my own and come into a new level of independence, which was just what I wanted. Less than two years later, divorce looked like my next solution. Even if I believed at that time that divorce was a bad thing, it was perfect for who I was and what I wanted. That brief marriage was a good example of discovering what I didn't want in life and then changing things – although not in the easiest manner. The pain of divorce, even without children and without a owning a house to divide, still overwhelmed both of us. Because that was so hard, I vowed my next marriage would be for life. I would marry the right person, and I would do my part to make it work. So I learned the hard way that time, but then the situation served more than one purpose. So be it.

In my youth were the days with drugs and alcohol and as much sex as we could get. There were rare moments when I deeply connected with someone. I loved those precious moments and wanted more. There were teachers who listened and cared. There were counselors who truly cared and helped.

Being open, malleable and having the flexibility to change is one factor in my success. While sitting in my car, waiting to pick up a friend at the San Francisco Airport. I sat quietly, watching the grasses right in front of me bending in the wind. Not one snapped like a tree in a storm. The grasses reminded me how when I am easy going, bending with the wind, I always bounce back.

In my very satisfying career as a schoolteacher and college professor, I was totally into my work. Once I retired, my life changed dramatically. I never thought I would have a home office or have my own practice. Eventually, I just chose not to work for others. Working for myself empowers me. I never thought I could be as happy and satisfied with life as I have been. I never thought it possible to have the satisfying thirty-year marriage that I have today. I just did not expect life to be so good. Just goes to show the power of questioning, flexibility, seeking, surrender and perseverance.

Chapter 19
Greatness

G reatness Circle, a relatively new activity in my life, transformed my ability to recognize and embrace my positive traits. Greatness Circle is a gathering of people committed to personal growth. For me it has been indispensable in my process of moving from a place of powerlessness to an empowered life. It happens gracefully, naturally. The group I go to meets in the Phoenix metro area.

Greatness Circle was created by two counselors who trained with Howard Glasser in Tucson, Arizona, in his Nurtured Heart Approach for helping children. He shared that he had noticed the approach he developed to help children was actually in great need by adults too. He talks about it in his book, *You are Oprah*. Those counselors started Greatness Circle and it is spreading. Through attending Greatness, my own growth expanded. I let go of minimizing myself and began acknowledging my greatness. At first I had to work hard to think of a greatness to share. I would chant on my way to Greatness Circle to be sure I could think of a greatness that merited sharing, or that was the best one I could come up with. Then, in less than a year, I changed. Now I often identify multiple greatnesses before I get to the Circle, and I have to decide which one to share. I sometimes see that multiple greatnesses really lie under the arch of something bigger that I hadn't seen before. Everyone who attends regularly evolves before our eyes. Sometimes when I share, people are moved to tears. I choke up too as others share or I get that goose bump feeling of "Aha: this is a truth I'm hearing."

Today, I know I always have greatness. I always did have it. I just didn't know it. My greatness is multifaceted, deep and always part of me.

In Greatness Circle, after a person shares their greatness, we, when inspired to do so, give supportive feedback. We reinforce that greatness for the person or offer additional specific kinds of greatness that we heard, saw, or felt that hadn't been mentioned yet. Affirmation and validation are powerful. To hear you are great because... and to know that the others are being really genuine, is a life changer. Some people, me included, were uncomfortable at first. Others fear they are bragging, and our cultural norms discourage bragging. But Greatness Circle is done differently. It is an authentic recognition of the truth of who we are and embracing it. It is good for us.

Today I stand in power, in awareness; it has been hard won, earned. I know there is more to come. I'm still here, am I not? Today I have the tools to heal myself and others. Today I know where to go.

My spiritual practice, albeit imperfect, means I get up each day, drink my apple-cider vinegar water or lemon water, and sit to meditate, sometimes with music or a guided meditation and more often without. Sometimes I pause, journal what comes up – maybe an insight, awareness, and pieces of the puzzle coming together and making more sense than before – seeing a bigger picture. Sometimes it comes as a realization that I'm holding on to someone, something, some belief that has outlived its time and has bubbled to the surface to be resolved. I also love playing uplifting music: Christian music that is about the bliss of knowing God, or I listen to Tibetan chants and at other times I enjoy what the Sikhs have put on You Tube.

And very importantly, I check in with myself and with Creator throughout the day, and stay open to new direction and new opportunities. I pray often, and as I see a need (especially for people on the streets and for horses in pens). I send light to others and fill myself with it. I listen when I sense guidance. I meditate again if I need it/want it. I read books that feed my spiritual growth. I give service when opportunity arises. I remember to take care of myself, and I care for my husband, too with clean clothes, good meals, attention and love. This keeps our home running smoothly and keeps me serene.

My spiritual practice has changed from a morning activity (meditation or chanting) and daily spontaneous prayer, to a full-time focus on living connected to the higher states of consciousness; always being aware that I have the support of the universe. Of course I do none of this perfectly; still, I keep plodding along and enjoying the benefits. I know I am not alone, and I always open myself to see us as the light beings that we already are. Enlightenment is my goal; meditation the road.

Chapter 20
Manifesting

Talking about manifesting is all the rage since the documentary The Secret came out in 2006. I have friends who pursue greater skill at it. I teach a popular ThetaHealing® class on it: Manifesting and Abundance. Manifesting is easy when what you want is part of your divine plan, as it was for me to become a teacher, a counselor, or to marry a particular person. It gets complicated when we say we want abundance but at the same time unconsciously block it.

The solution for me includes focus, intentionality, and perseverance, and more recently, learning to identify the beliefs and patterns that held me back. For instance, it appeared that my family (both sides), although not living in poverty, carried a genetic program for it, very likely in part because my grandparents lived during the Great Depression. I also carried religious vows of poverty from previous lives. With ThetaHealing®, I released the programs and vows. Today I believe my financial future is wide open to attracting abundance. I regularly see evidence, which often appears from unexpected sources. With ThetaHealing®, I released what had held me back.

For a long while I've believed all the intense negative karma I intended to experience and clear in this life was bunched up in my first twenty-five years, ending with my mother's murder. Since then, life has been much, much easier:

no drama, no trauma, just the regular ups and downs. I decided a long time ago that I intend to live a spiritually focused, peaceful life. Sure, I still hike the Grand Canyon and play beach volleyball; I just have no tolerance for drama or for dysfunction in my friendships, so I choose carefully who is in my life.

Perseverance and determination serve me as deeply ingrained traits that enable me to create the life I want. It doesn't mean I don't ever quit anything; it is just the important stuff, like emotional growth, inner freedom and awareness that I go after until I have what I want.

Focus comes easiest if I add the structure I need. It may be related to working in a school system for over thirty years; I need regular goal setting and due dates. When I have a choice, I prefer structured programs because they guide me to success. On my own, I'll procrastinate.

Intentionality is powerful. I know intention and desire isn't the Buddhist way. In their paradigm, we release all desires in order to gain enlightenment and true happiness. In the meantime, I allow my desires to propel me towards the change, the gifts, and the life I want.

Today, I allow myself bigger dreams than ever. New possibilities are within reach. I do the work, remove my blocks, and open the door to optimism, increased financial success, happiness and self-realization.

Chapter 21
Being

I avoided myself and my emotional pain by working and going to college for my bachelor's in special education and partying. Well, for financial independence too. I worked as a cocktail waitress, a school bus driver, at the state institution and as a camp counselor while in college. After I became a teacher, I volunteered, I tutored, and I worked the land (at our Christian/New age commune in Oregon). Then I went after a Master's degree in special education while working full time. I earned a principal's certificate and a substance-abuse counseling license too, while working full time. After that I continued to teach and to earn a doctorate without taking a leave of absence, completing it in two and a half years. I think you get the picture. I then continued to teach full time, worked in drug treatment part time, taught for the university part time and taught meditation classes on occasion too. Burnout approached. In some circles this is called workaholism.

In my last years before retiring from the school district, I dropped the job in drug treatment and continued with the university part time. I gained weight, and I was so unhappy the last three years I taught in the public schools. I was dissatisfied with the system and not the wonderful teacher I was used to being. I just didn't have it in me anymore. After retirement, I continued to teach for the university where I had the pleasure of helping others become special-education teachers. Those were my favorite classes to teach, my world (schools), my people (teachers). My commitment to the children I had taught was still in my heart, and I could feed that love for kids and learning by teaching others how to be skilled, knowledgeable, compassionate teachers too.

That is my personal example of doing. It took a toll. Today I work for myself, and I set the pace that feels just right. Having interests, stimulation, learning, and love without too much busyness feels balanced and stressless.

There are blends of Doing and Being that work. There is purpose in action/doing.

Beingness found in meditation, in stillness, in God, calls me. Chanting, studying the words of spiritual teachers and masters, and journaling usher me to the state of just Being.

I've read that when people give up an addiction, many who are successful pick up a new habit, a habit for which it doesn't matter if it moves to an obsessive/compulsive (addiction) level. Two were listed. One was meditating; the other was running. Two very different behaviors that have a similar effect on the mind.

What matters in life usually is living in balance. Most likely I taught the Being versus Doing workshops because it is what I needed to learn. Obviously I overdid doing. I want what feeds my soul and brings lightness. For me, the goal is now to do as much as possible from the Being state and ultimately everything while in the Being state.

In the workshops I would create this model Venn diagram to show and discuss what is the state of Being and what is Doing. Then the attendees would create their own and set a personal goal to add more Being time or more Doing while Being activities. The one below is an example of mine now. I have included a blank Venn Diagram at the back of the book for considering how much time you spend Being or Doing. If you choose to fill it out, after it is done, you can decide if it would serve you to have more Being in life or more Being with Doing.

A Human Doing and A Human Being

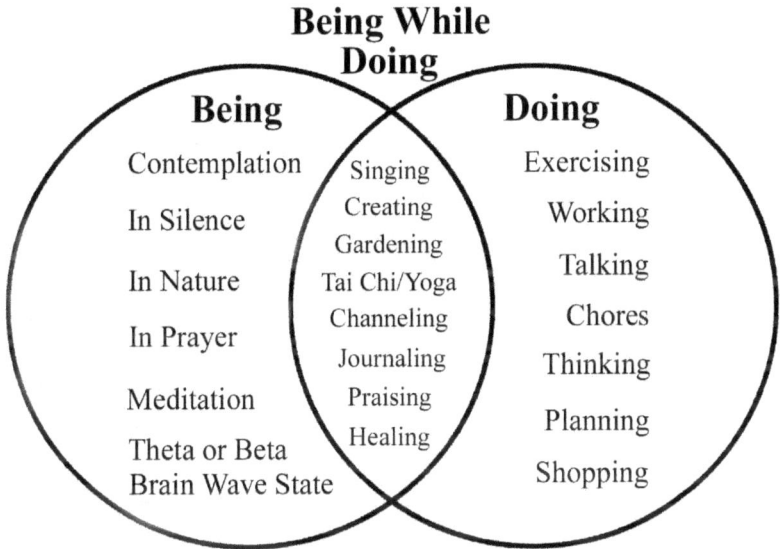

Being While Doing

Being

Contemplation

In Silence

In Nature

In Prayer

Meditation

Theta or Beta
Brain Wave State

Singing
Creating
Gardening
Tai Chi/Yoga
Channeling
Journaling
Praising
Healing

Doing

Exercising

Working

Talking

Chores

Thinking

Planning

Shopping

Chapter 22
Letting Go

While writing this book, I gave up caffeine. I was surprised how easy it was. One morning I had a headache: that's all. I healed it and moved on. Now I am caffeine free and having a new experience each morning, with no artificial energy jolts needed to get me going, and less tension in my face and shoulders from caffeine. No longer driven by caffeine addiction, it's freeing!

As I grow and change, my world does too. I don't attract certain kinds of situations anymore. There was a time when I was overwhelmed by the number of kitties, doggies, deer, rabbits etc. (you get the idea of animals) dead on the road or on the side of the road. Something changed, and that just stopped happening. I go for long periods of time without seeing that now. It does happen; yet it is pleasantly infrequent. How did that happen? Something must have shifted inside, so it was no longer necessary for me to have that that experience.

It's funny, but just this week I prayed to have God remove the belief that I attract pain-filled scenes around me. That was because of the pain I take in from others when I see suffering – such as a child crying and being ignored by the parent in the store, or a dog lost and running by the highway. I want to free myself further from the need to attract the things that will cause me to re-experience pain and grief.

I look for what I can do to release that need, such as clearing vows to relieve suffering in the world. I've released them because I want it to be a conscious choice when I can and do release suffering from others. That is what happens as I work with clients. I don't need to suffer along with people. I don't need to attract it so I can heal it. I can be aware of it, and assist others to release it, but I don't have to feel it as deeply as I did.

Geesh, I remember when I was teaching school, and kids would rush in to show me their latest wound, pull up the Band-Aid or a t-shirt and show me a gash. Oh, the pain was immediate in my body. I no longer have to feel their pain in my body. It isn't a vow now (thanks to ThetaHealing®); it is a choice. I want to relieve suffering for others, just as others have helped me with it. I no longer have to experience it with them.

Negative self-talk, another trait to let go (my current focus), catch it quick and erase, delete and replace with a positive.

Also, I wish to continue releasing the need for permanence, the need to hold on tightly. Nothing is permanent: plants blossom then wilt, people pass on, friends move away, our stuff breaks, and so it goes. So I practice nonattachment, another Buddhist practice; just letting go. Letting go, surrender and acceptance challenge rigidity, stuckness and suffering. Releasing old things and beliefs creates the freedom most people seek.

Chapter 23
Change

B eing motivated, keeping the determination I found in myself to go for the things I'm passionate about: growth, teaching, healing, travel, and deep connection with like-minded humans, helped me create the life I wanted. Truly, I think persevering means that anything is possible.

I became motivated to change an unhealthy pattern when I met my husband-to-be. At first, I reverted to an old, negative response to men after a few dates. When I discovered he really liked me, I intended to send him on his way through nonverbal cues, not saying anything directly. As he shied away from our relationship, I realized I didn't want to lose him. I decided to change my ways (to allow a decent guy to like me) so I could have this person in my life. It was so worth it. We have a thirty-plus-year marriage now. Of course, I didn't know where it was headed back then. I just knew that I wanted to keep him around. He was smart, moral and very much what I wanted in my life. He was worth my changing. I was motivated.

At other times I've felt stuck. I knew grief overwhelmed me; burnout in public school teaching approached and I couldn't do anything about any of it. Yuck. I didn't like it and I didn't know how to get out. Allowing some time between changes is necessary, as are transitions, rest periods, and time to integrate new ideas. But when it felt as if I was stuck and unhappy, it really troubled me.

One thing I did was to study people I liked and who appeared to do well in life. One, a girlfriend I taught elementary school with, showed graciousness in so many social settings. From her, I learned to thank people and let them know when they helped. I integrated some of her skills into my daily life, just to make socializing and friendships smoother.

Also, as I said, I'd read self-help books AND did the exercises in them. When therapists gave me homework, I did it and reported back. Apparently it is my nature to seek change and growth, including moving regularly and changing jobs. Essentially, changing within, freeing myself is really what I'm talking about: change as growth and expansion.

Recently (and rather abruptly) I noticed that I was still allowing people who are hurtful to remain in my life. Even though my life improved in many ways, an old pattern reappeared. I'm human. I'm much quicker now to catch it, process what is going on, then let that person go or make the next change that is right for me.

After my dad died (from the fire), my mom chose two successive husbands who threatened her or hit her. Her own stepfather had beaten her. How could she have chosen differently when she was an adult? She could have decided on a different way of life for herself if she had rejected her parents' life lessons. Because of the losses she experienced in the house fire when she was just twenty-six, I don't think that option stayed in place for her. She continued to live the pain of being stuck and repeating dysfunctional family patterns.

Although I feel stuck at times, I don't stay stuck. I am malleable. I overcome limitations. I thought Thich Nhat Hanh said it well in *No Mud, No Lotus: The Art of Transforming Suffering*, "We're also able to go further and transform our suffering into understanding, compassion, and joy for ourselves and for others."

Chapter 24
Karma

I think it is interesting that in my early thirties I did a self-inventory, and mostly came up with what others had done to me. I still lived in a victim mentality. At that time I thought I had no responsibility in the events in my life, or only a little. Today I see everything in my life, including the traumas and tragedies, as experiences that I brought to myself for various reasons (truly all based on karma).

Here is an example of how my understanding expanded from being a victim to knowing every event in my life has a cause. My view eventually changed of the rape I went through when I was thirteen, at the hands of four young men, in the back of a station wagon in the Nevada desert north of Reno. The karma, the cause of the trauma, was revealed to me in a dream. The dream I recognized as a past-life memory of being a slave-ship worker with some status, because I had the right to take captives and have sex with them at my will. I don't know in that life how many women and boys had sated my appetite, but it was ugly. I was an ugly being at that time. People were drowned for various reasons, but I didn't have qualms about it then. When I remembered all that, I actually felt a sense of relief that I had had the horrific encounter at age thirteen, and that my atonement for the actions in another life was complete. Granted, moving to forgiveness of the men involved came later, gradually, but there was that precise day when I was okay with what had happened to me, and I was grateful that I had atoned.

I think most of the reason we don't remember that we set these things in place for a lifetime is if we could see it coming, we would say, "No. No way. I'm not doing that or undergoing that." Then we'd do everything in our power to avoid the consequence for a previous action. We would deny ourselves the opportunity to clear karma, thinking, "I'm in the physical now; I can't tolerate that." So before we are born, we set ourselves up for what is in our highest and best interest, and go with that (and drop the conscious awareness of it after incarnating). When the time comes (when it all hits the fan), we say "What?" or "What the f…?" Yet amazingly, all in good time, we can come to peace with anything. Once the karma is cleared, all that transpired remains as a memory.

As I said, I was raped by four men in the desert. I was powerless at that age to have stopped them. I carried that sense of powerlessness for another ten-plus years. I wish I could have reported it then, so that possibly, after their arrests, others could have been protected. I was too humiliated, shamed, and bewildered, and I feared the threats of death from the group's leader. I didn't report it for over twenty years. I waited until after I felt safe; until I was married, got therapy, and had lots of wonderfully supportive people around me. The guy who was the leader the night of the rape had just gotten out of prison. It is my sincere wish he got sent back. My intuition tells me he hurt a lot of other women, and killed, too. He so convincingly threatened my life that I was paralyzed with fear by the things he said he'd do to me if I reported them.

To clarify, I set up my life to put people and events in at the right times to propel me to either release karma or to teach me something, or to even create a desire for something. Probaby that is what everyone does. I used lots of resources to heal and mature, and I never gave up.

Here's an example in someone else's life: My friend married, had kids and came to regret that the man she married was horrible to their children. Maybe this situation is perfect too, because the children had karma with those parents that they wanted to experience, and it was provided with those particular parents. The children's purpose in selecting this particular family was a factor, and the mother finds accepting all of that challenging.

As a personal example, I worked with a department head in a middle school; she thwarted my efforts to provide materials for my students several years in a row. I was frustrated, angry, and blaming. Once someone asked me who she reminded me of, and I realized how much she looked like and reminded me of my mother. Then I was able to begin the process of healing my relationship with my mother. Ultimately, the situation resolved until I didn't have any emotions about the woman at work. Also, I didn't have to do anything regarding the woman to fix the lack of materials problem. I had to work on my mother issues. As they resolved, the work problem did too. That coworker was the perfect person at that time to trigger a new stage of growth and healing for me. Of course I did not see it that way at first.

Around that time, I learned the prayer used by people in many twelve-step programs: When someone is upsetting you, on your mind repeatedly, and you can't accept them or what they do or did, do this: Pray for (name the person here)'s health, happiness and prosperity. Pray for yourself, asking for love, compassion and understanding. This powerful prayer frequently brings amazing results.

The changes in thinking, self-understanding, self-acceptance and eliminating the victim viewpoint came about through therapy, study, meditation, ThetaHealing®, journaling, persevering, seeking, and people wiser than me who listened and listened and listened.

My understanding of my karma and its purpose has changed. Originally I thought enduring the karmic requirements of my first twenty-five years (near-death experience, rape, abuse and my mother's murder) meant that cleaning up my karma was the point. And that is most likely still true. At this time, I came to a larger perspective; maybe I chose to release all that karma by age twenty-five, while at the same time I chose to bring all of that into my life – so I would have the depth of compassion for others, so I would have to turn to God, so I would choose to live a life of service to humanity. Maybe I chose to process all that karma in twenty-five years for all those benefits, too. Maybe it was a really good thing.

Chapter 25
Know Yourself

I hear that some people have a sense of belonging and feel as though they fit in. I never did. I always felt different, unique, and alone. I sought ways to explain why that was.

I took the Myers-Briggs Personality Inventory, hoping to understand myself better. It let me know I can be both introverted and extraverted; sensing, feeling, and judging. The results and descriptions offered some validation of what I've known about myself, and explained more.

Again seeking a better understanding of myself, I read Dan Millman's book titled *The Life You Were Meant to Live*. It told me I am a "9": here to trust and follow Spirit manifesting within. It says people like me excel in service and healing-related work, and that everything is more meaningful to us if connected to a higher purpose. It validated me and offered me insight.

I've used Louise Hay's book *You Can Heal Your Life* for years now, because in it, she explains how each ailment symbolizes who we are internally, who we believe we are, who and what we are afraid of. She explains that we use illness as a vehicle to show us what needs to change in our lives. Stiffness in the neck means unwillingness to flex. Bad eyes tell us there is something we don't want to see. Hearing loss indicates there is something we don't want to hear. A sore throat suggests hurting yourself by not speaking your truth. Problems in the digestive tract relate to undigested ideas and difficulty digesting new ideas in life.

Her work is amazing, as is Inna Segal, and her guide *The Secret Language of Your Body*. They showed me how to recognize and understand that the symptoms in bodies have purpose. The symptoms that develop are shaped by our thoughts, beliefs, emotions and fears. These can heal through non-medical means if the limiting beliefs are discovered and released, as we talked about, with ThetaHealing®. No need to stay in pain: there is relief at hand.

Louise Hay and Inna Segal's books helped me gain awareness that poor health alerts us to the need for change. It sends us signals that it's time to pay attention.

I took my first meditation class when I was nineteen. It is evident that it changed me. Insight Meditation is probably what I've practiced the most. One of my favorite Buddhist meditation teachers, Jack Kornfield, explains meditation well. His books and conferences helped me along the way. I especially loved *After the Ecstasy, the Laundry.* Change through meditation is a gradual, incremental process. It gets easier; still my mind will babble after thirty-five years of meditation. Okay, to be honest, I wasn't a consistent meditator for decades. The last decade has been the most consistent and much easier. In fact, it is so wonderful, I wonder why I stop, get up and start my day. That, though, is the human condition.

In Oregon my spiritual teachers, Nancy Ottis and the Reverends Martha and Harold Hicks, guided me to find my higher self, to channel, and to continue to develop a daily spiritual practice. I used activities from the *Seth* books by Jane Roberts, and Sanaya Roman and Duane Packer's book *Opening to Channel,* also Sanaya Roman's book *Spiritual Growth: Being your Higher Self.*

Today I only channel by first going to Source, in order to be certain I am very connected with God. That way, I can trust the information to be of the highest level. That's critical. I don't want to be put in a bad position or to share any limited truths, which can happen if the entity isn't contacted through God. I changed how I channeled, once I learned the difference in technique.

Chapter 26
Seeing Clearly

The kind of praying I did as a child proved ineffective. I'd pray, "God, please make my mom not drink so much and to come home more. Please get me a loving dad like my real dad." With frustration, I discovered I couldn't change people or make things happen with people. Over time, I found I could change myself. I have continued to change myself until I see the perfection of everything as it is. Okay, it took some years.

Eventually, through study and meditation, I have come to live with an understanding that all of us always have been, and always will be. We are eternal. I am empowered by that unseen force, the Creator, the universe, which, for example, sends angels to talk to children in hospitals. At least that was an experience I had while sitting in my crib in the hospital after the fire. Two blue angels came and talked with me when I was alone. I can't tell you when or why. I just know that they made me happy. I was really grateful for their presence. It eased the loneliness.

Today I live in a good neighborhood, have a lovely little house with a pool that my husband and I enjoy. I've added to the vibrations of the house so that when clients and students come over, they love the energy and feel peaceful. Our home is our sanctuary.

Earlier, I mentioned removing toxic people from my life who may have had a purpose in it at one time, but not now.

They became hurtful too often, or the damage that they liked to inflict (or maybe unknowingly inflicted) was such that I wouldn't have it any more. It is healthy to let go of the people who are not true friends, who don't love you the way you can be loved.

One example that took many years to see all the way through is the letting go of a spiritual teacher. I studied with a woman, a minister, then, when she opened a commune, I lived with her and the members of that group for years. I studied under her again for years, after I married and had moved out. She professed to care about me; maybe she did. But the truth is that I grew and grew, and she chose to stay the same. She avoided this healing and growth work I talk about; she said it was too painful for her. She developed spiritually, yet didn't heal her past. She stayed away from the deep inner hurt by immersing herself in spiritual activities and later her church. At the same time, she hurt me and others, and apparently couldn't stop herself. Another member and I talked with her about it. We asked for change from her, and in how she did things with the group. She just couldn't. Finally I went my separate way. She blames me that the group disintegrated after that.

Ah, there's that word blame again. It is important that I learned that when I blame another person, I'm not taking responsibility for what I have created in my own life. Now, when I hear myself blaming someone, I know I have to stop, examine the situation and look for my responsibility in it. When others blame me, I check myself for the veracity of it, and unless I am truly responsible, I just let it go. I can ignore how they feel about me. It's not my business.

I'd like to add that although a time came to release this woman as my teacher, and the process was challenging, I want to acknowledge the positive influence and the many spiritual gifts she led me to. She encouraged me to have a regular meditation practice, put books in my hands, and took me to the church where I went back and received the Holy Spirit. She introduced me to the man who became my husband. She guided me from my youth and dangerous activities to stability. She nurtured the seeker in me. More than likely that relationship even though quite tiresome in the end was full of purpose and value, exactly as it needed to be for both of us.

My experience with the minister is also a good example of something else I want to share. I realized quite a while back that I haven't seen people accurately. Of course, that is because I didn't see myself accurately. I used to put people on pedestals and think they are better than me. This is especially true when they have spiritual attributes. This was an unhealthy practice that was a disservice to both me and the other person. Today, any time I think anyone is more special or more gifted than most of us, I see it as a signal to do more work on myself. It means it is time to identify why I am assessing the person that way. It isn't about the person; it is about my own thoughts and beliefs.

I've met many wonderful spiritual teachers who were in denial, or in pain, or stuck. They had so much spirituality, with amazing gifts: from levitation to the ability to hear guidance for themselves and others, high vibrations, the ability to attract students, and the ability to guide their students well. Originally I thought they had what I wanted, but as clarity came, I saw the limitations. They still had so much work to do. I think it is a reflection of me, and a rejection of what I didn't want to see about me. I am a spiritual beauty and was an emotional wreck. Putting others on a pedestal probably happened because I expected perfection from myself, and I used the black-and-white thinking that others are perfect and I am not. This thinking had a degree of immaturity to it, and it deserved questioning.

In my forties, I met a handsome Buddhist monk who appeared to be in great emotional pain. He showed me that even really gifted spiritual people can still experience deep pain, and not find a solution in themselves. It was a greater force that saved him from suicide. As he told me about that event, it looked as though, from the day of that spiritual intervention, he moved forward, the grief and anguish passed, and he regained the ability to teach again.

I wonder who else I'll meet along the path.

Chapter 27
Multitude of Ways

Just two and a half years ago I learned about downloads: a New Age healing technique that is growing in popularity. I like them because they are so, so effortless. In ThetaHealing®, we ask Creator to give us the downloads we need, such as positive beliefs – new and higher perspectives that move us into new ways of thinking and open whole new areas of possibility. For instance, I might request downloads like: I write with grace and ease, I recognize my own self-worth, I know when to and how to articulate my feelings. There are tens of thousands of downloads. Downloads are absorbed more quickly than affirmations. I still use affirmations occasionally, though when I want to focus on a particular message or goal, I write them in my weekly planner so I see it frequently. Downloads come directly from Source; this way, we are co-creating a new reality for ourselves with Creator. Creator loves us so much that it gives all that and more.

Here are a few more examples: I have Creator's perspective on what intimacy is. I know what it feels like to live without regret. I know what the Creator's definition of forgiveness feels like. I know how to live in joy.

Visualization is also a positive practice tool that I use frequently while going to sleep. In those minutes, I create what I want in my life by seeing it, expanding it, feeling it and enjoying. Lately I've been visualizing the house I want to have at the beach. In that process, I realize I want to live there for forty years or so, and if it is near the beach, the rising tides will create problems – so I changed my picture to a house on the side of a hill overlooking the beach. Besides seeing all the details the way I'd like them, I add good feelings, too.

All these tools and actions referred to in this book are just a fraction of the healing programs, spiritual masters and great self-help books available. It is not necessary to be religious or to spend great amounts of money. The key lies in finding what works and doing that until the next right thing or teacher comes along. As they say it is a process. We can trust ourselves and the universe to provide what we need at the right time.

Chapter 28

Trust

I used to fear I wouldn't choose what is best for me. I'd made choices that hurt me. I didn't trust myself. All the self-help books, therapy and recovery work improved that. I may still check in with my husband and get his advice on something, but I am not afraid to make decisions. I trust myself – and it feels good.

My father-in-law showed me, although I had experienced abuse from other father figures in the past, that not all males were that way. Some older men could be trusted. He was one.

After living with my second stepdad and his alcohol, anger and masculinity issues; after being with my grandfather (maternal) and his inappropriate touching and alcohol abuse; and as I already told you about my other relative with alcohol and pedophilia; I couldn't trust men. There was also a great-uncle who just couldn't keep his hands to himself. He was always grabbing my butt or breast. Creep. Obviously my take-away from all that was that men weren't trustworthy, period.

The first time I was alone with my father-in-law, I was terrified that some violation would happen again. It didn't matter that I was twenty-nine years old. Terror ruled my mind. I baked a cake that night and waited for the worst. I went into the den to sit and watch TV with him. He fell asleep. I read a magazine. When my husband and mother-in-law got home, all was calm. My worst fears never materialized.

Through him, my God showed me that the world is safer than I thought. As the years went by, my father-in-law and I went for walks together and talked. Boy, do I miss this man. We refinished some pieces of furniture together: that, too, was a new experience. I got to work on projects with a father figure, and I had fun, and I even got bored, because I expected the worst. With Dad (my father-in-law) there was no drama. No yelling. No hitting. No name calling. Nothing sexual. No need for running away.

Well, actually, I walked away from one project, waiting for the finish on a piece of furniture to dry, because I was emotionally and physically geared up for drama and there just wasn't any. It was a new experience for me, realizing that people can work with each other without tensions. I'm so glad I learned it was possible through him. He is gone now, and both my husband and I miss him dearly.

As I write this, I see that being with my husband couldn't teach me what the time with my father-in-law did. My husband is a safe male, but he wasn't a father figure. I needed to see that an older male could be a decent human being.

Chapter 29
Forgiveness

Forgiveness is difficult. I didn't worry about attempting it for years. I didn't want to force it on myself, although I always found if I did the internal work gradually, I naturally came to forgiveness. Still, I was patient and gentle with myself with that work. I do not carry a grudge or resentments about the physical, sexual or emotional abuse now, even for my other relatives, my mom or my stepfather. I know what happened. I know I was hurt. Others were hurt, too. I live free of that emotional pain today.

The work required to heal and eventually forgive each person going back again and again and finding what was left and finding out whom I still resented. That hurt too, and it took years. I used ThetaHealing® during the last three years, and therapists and other tools before that. I can talk about the abuse with so much less grief and anger now.

Forgiving me took the longest. At first I didn't even know what I'd need to forgive myself for. Ultimately I had a list, and could process my way through it. Now when things come up and I get mad or frustrated with myself, I can work through and release them much faster than before. Yeah.

I do not remember who lectured me on needing to forgive right now, saying that it was the Christian thing to do. I was pretty young and the result of that conversation was kick starting that stubborn part of me that refused to forgive until I was ready. Consequently, I believe in gently encouraging forgiveness. Complete forgiveness appears to be an incremental process. Allowing it to come in due time, then with loving kindness moving through each stage until clear and complete turned out most effective for me.

Chapter 30
Sacrifice

S ome people's visions I have heard described lasted for hours. Mine usually are a flash. I will see a single scene and get understanding and be deeply affected by the meaning. It usually carries a big "aha" kind of feeling with it. The visions are not something I control. They come when it is relevant. The vision and its message is my truth at the time it comes. My spiritual development also grows, so that what was meaningful and made sense at one time changes to a much broader picture or higher perspective later.

During a massage following a mud bath in Calistoga, California, with my eyes closed, I saw Christ kneeling against the rock and I understood sacrifice (Christ in Gethsemane) as I never had before. It connected with the life I remember when I sacrificed myself right on into the volcano for the village. I was pleased to have the honor of being selected and I believed I was saving them.

There is another life I remembered where I was happy to sacrifice myself for the people of the land I loved, because God had given me a vision. I believed I could to save those people, protect their right to their land, and vanquish the usurpers. Through ThetaHealing®, I came to understand I had a sacrifice program running for centuries. Then I released it, because now I see sacrifice has been a spiritual gift to humanity, yet is no longer necessary. It appeared to be, until recently, a karmic requirement to sacrifice ourselves to make a difference. Today we don't have to sacrifice ourselves. We by choice take a mission, and step out of safety to help others, but we don't have to become a sacrifice to achieve something meaningful

In 1958, remarkably, my father sacrificed his life saving me from the fire. He grabbed me from my crib and carried me out of the burning house. I was found on the front lawn. But he sacrificed again and again, trying to reach his other two daughters and to get them out of our burning home. In the end, he died in the hospital from his burns. His other two daughters, my sisters age six and eight, also died. I truly believe it was worth it to him. Most parents would do the same.

Saving me, and sacrificing his life for his daughters, show the savior and sacrifice programs (genetic and soul level beliefs) run in my family. I've released myself from it (through ThetaHealing® again). My dad accomplished his purpose in those events. What a difficult and painful way to fulfill desire (karma)!

I hope I don't sound too tough or too cold, or as though I have no feelings. I choose to direct my life through my choices not to be compelled by beliefs that force me to sacrifice. I can be of service without sacrifice. I was overwhelmed the majority of my life by feelings of grief and fear from all the traumas. I have done enough of the healing work that I can talk about the events and the people with just occasional emotion. What a relief to have such a huge benefit from doing the personal work – to move from suffering to understanding, acceptance and inner peace.

Chapter 31
Teachers

I have noticed how I brought a large number of people into my life as teachers, people who would influence me in a particular direction. For example, when I chose my Uncle Lee, a school principal, it was to create influence from family members, causing me in turn to want to become a teacher, and later to want to be a principal, too. Also, I chose him to be in my life (I started spending as much time as I could with him once I was an adult) so I could see that the man closest to my father was a wonderful man, with whom I was always safe. He was someone I could trust and respect.

Also, I think there was a relationship between seeing a therapist in ninth grade (I had started running away from home) and years later, when I would get a counseling license and work in drug treatment, reaching people who didn't believe in themselves or trust themselves. After I had worked with that first therapist, I wanted to become a psychiatrist. I read the books the therapist recommended, and learned about psychology and human nature. It was so helpful. It made the world make a little more sense. I even got to help children in the schools where I taught, through talking (counseling) circles/groups, and again when a few children came to me to report abuse they were experiencing. Loving psychology and counseling served me well. I have already talked about my paternal grandmother and the great power of her unconditional love; that along with rules and structure were positive forces in my life. Resilience research says a significant person in a child's life can make all the difference between a fulfilling life and failure. She is the one I identified as most significant in my life.

One of my amazing husband's greatest gifts to me was when he showed me I am lovable and already deeply loved. Originally I really did not know this. I bring this up because I believe in the power of bringing teachers into your life.

In the first few years of our marriage, he would ask me before he left for work, "Who loves you?" Apparently he knew I did not know I was loved at all. He would wait for me to answer. At first, I could only say Jesus does. It was the only thing I was sure of. I wondered if others might – or maybe not. Then I eventually could include my cat. Each time he would ask, he would wait and give me a chance to come up with a few more people who loved me. In due course, I could recite a short list to his question. Then as days, weeks, months went by, the list grew to include Jesus, him (my husband), and my cat, my sister and a few others. It became easier and easier. I am so grateful he knew to do this for me, that he persisted until I had a good grasp on the fact that I am loved. I am also grateful for his presence in my life for thirty-plus really good years now.

He even put a note in my grocery bag for the most recent retreat I attended, stating "Remember who loves you." That is unconditional love.

I wonder how much Mom's relationship with me (and all the hurt I took from it that I later saw as useful) was actually possibly her sacrifice too.

I used James Redfield's book *The Celestine Prophecy* to guide me when I wanted to improve my understanding of my parent's roles in my life. He explained the nine insights. The one about understanding the meaning that each of your parents' lives has for you, caused me to ask, "What did they teach me?

What was I with them to learn about life?" His work influenced my discovery and understanding that each parent had a distinct purpose, which molded my life and influenced the development of my primary spiritual purpose today.

My understanding has morphed several times, and it is now at the level I talked about in Chapter One. I understand my mother's inability to show and give as much love as I wanted was a gift that caused me to search for love – and I found that humans just didn't have as much as I wanted. From there, I found it is God who has the love I want. It is reliable, permanent, and more deeply satisfying, than any other love I've known.

Because of my husband and my seeking of God, I came to see love in a new light and came to recognize all have it. Love is everywhere, easily found. The gradual change in my awareness allowed me to see it, know it and feel it.

Chapter 32
Depression

A fter college, and while in my first teaching job, I studied psychology; again looking for explanations. A few different therapists helped too. Not so much when they said "you're depressed," but because I took that information and researched depression, and saw that I was one of the one in ten Americans who are depressed – and that I'd spent most of my life that way. After that, many of the ridiculous things I had done as a teen (sneaking alcohol, crying a lot, and not washing my hair) and in college (drinking and using) made sense. It makes sense in light of all the losses, from my dad and sisters when I was two, to the loss of my mother in a robbery of her bar when I was twenty-five. Yes, I could see I was depressed for good reason. There was a while there when, besides seeking teachers and positive ways to understand the world, I self-medicated to numb myself to my grief, shame and fear.

In my thirties, while creating a genogram (a diagram outlining the history of the behavior patterns of a family over several generations) for a substance-abuse counseling class I took to earn a counseling license, I put more of the pieces together. Details came to light: for instance, my paternal grandfather had committed suicide after the "Great Depression," the failure of his farm, a divorce, and the loss of his son and grandchildren in the house fire in 1958. What great grief he must have carried. The genogram showed me that depression was in my genetic code. Let's face it: I could have been depressed just through my experiences by age seven. The genogram also showed more dysfunctional family patterns of physical and sexual abuse, alcohol and religious dependence; the black sheep and the heroes. The light bulbs turned on. I thought, "Look at my family: alcoholism and abuse on both the paternal and maternal sides. Yikes!"

Renee Raimondi, a wonderful teacher-friend in my life for about ten years, told me that when you're depressed and you naturally don't want to do anything, do just one thing. It will help. Take just one action: call someone, read a meaningful book, watch a sad movie and cry, or watch a comedy and laugh. I trusted her and did it.

She also told me that anger is underlying the depression. At first I did not even know that I was repressing anger. Releasing the anger helps the depression automatically lift; that is, of course, if I'm not feeding it sugar and alcohol. So going deeper to discover the anger, the source of it; then healing and releasing it.

As I came out of my depression and was driving my sporty, white convertible through Scottsdale, Arizona on a lovely sunny day, I felt so much happiness, just joy with me and the people in my life and my little car and the music booming from the stereo system. I loved myself at that moment. Then I freaked and thought, "Oh no, I must be bipolar." No, really, I'm not, it was just fear, stemming from a combination of studying psychology and counseling and my old negative mind-set of not being used to a lighter, happier me. Ha.

Now I notice depression on occasion for part of day, and at worst a few days; it doesn't last. I think that is what people who haven't been depressed for years' experience: just movement of moods, some up, some down. What a relief, because depression still scares me. We just lost the entertainer,

Robin Williams to it, also my cousin's husband, a Vietnam Veteran, and so many more people than I will ever know. Depression, although powerful and devastating, fortunately was manageable for me.

Chapter 33
Love

I glimpsed the other day, while driving to a writing workshop in Sedona, that what I think of as life is not a hard-and-fast reality. As I drove and looked at a mileage sign, I remembered a moment just like it in a dream and wondered "Is this a dream too?" Then, as I looked out across the plateau next to the highway, the desert seemed to be falling away, reminding me of a piece of art showing a landscape, while out at the edge of it, it is falling away molecule by molecule. It illustrated that what I see isn't real. It was a fascinating, yet eerie feeling. I was attracted to it, and a bit scared, because I didn't know how far the falling away of the land would go and I was driving a car at eighty miles an hour. I relish, though, that momentary knowing that all of this life is only a construct, an illusion (somewhat like in the movie The Matrix). It is something created for a purpose, but it isn't actually real. Like a fort built for kids to create their imaginary world, and play out their fantasies and dreams, I created my world for my karma, for experience, for learning and to wake up to my God self.

The more I filled my bucket, and the more I did to repair the hole in the bottom of it, the better life got – and the more that moments of happiness and connection to source became my normal.

I am grateful that things have changed and are different than I thought when I was younger. Having releasing the need for traditional religion, I move towards enlightenment. I accepted Jesus and the Holy Spirit. I became Buddhist, then New Age and metaphysical. So this independent way of finding what I need, and persisting until I began to get inklings of peace – this is the right way for me.

The journey has been so worth it. To live, and only experience pain or depression infrequently: that's a good life. To have less self-doubt and to know what to do when the time for action or decision comes: that's a good life. To be a resource for others, to know I help others release the dross and embrace their light more than ever that's a great life. Life is rich with people; with connection; with meaning, direction and joy.

I am not alone. I always have hope. I have All That Is.

Steps: A check off list

- ☐ Take Action
- ☐ Read
- ☐ Pray
- ☐ Go within
- ☐ Meditate
- ☐ Expect a miracle
- ☐ Journal
- ☐ Search the internet
- ☐ Do things differently than before
- ☐ Create a mission statement
- ☐ Utilize resources, people, and tools
- ☐ Expect synchronicity
- ☐ Take up a new habit
- ☐ Talk to people
- ☐ Make a decision
- ☐ Set intention
- ☐ Challenge yourself
- ☐ Ask for a teacher in spirit to guide you
- ☐ Hire a coach
- ☐ Ask to become aware when angels are with you
- ☐ See a therapist
- ☐ Attend Greatness Circle
- ☐ Surrender
- ☐ Seek
- ☐ Create a vision board
- ☐ Attend Adult Children of Alcoholic/Dysfunctional families meetings (ACA)

- ☐ Use your awareness
- ☐ Discard what doesn't work
- ☐ Trust yourself
- ☐ Get out into nature
- ☐ Take a yoga, tai chi or qi gong class
- ☐ Get 3 people's input before making challenging decisions

This is the template I created for my Doing vs Being workshops. I've included an example in Chapter 21 similar to what I filled out while demonstrating in workshops and a blank one here for you to copy and use. After filling out the three columns as they apply to your life, you might want to set a goal to increase either the Being column or the Being with Doing column.

A Human Doing   or   A Human Being

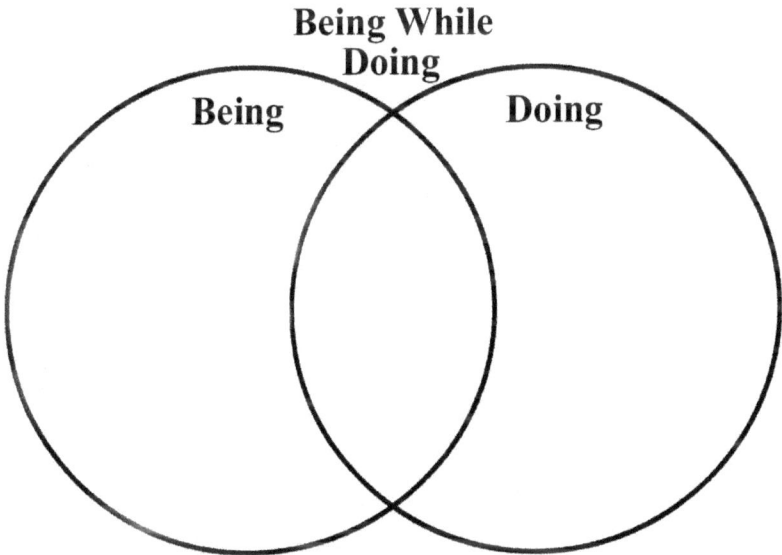

Being While Doing

Being   **Doing**

Resources:

Course in Miracles
www.DesertJewel.org
Greatness Circle, evokinggreatness@yahoo.com
Self-Realization Fellowship Lessons
Soka Gakkai International, www.sgi.org

Recommended Films:

Ghost
Interstellar
Lucy
Oh God
Matrix
What Dreams May Come

Recommended Reading:

Adult Children of Alcoholics Alcoholic/Dysfunctional Families,
2006 (also known as The Big Red Book)

Richard Bach, *One*, 1988

Ellen Bass and Laura Davis, *The Courage to Heal*: A Guide for
Women Survivors of Child Sexual Abuse, 20th Anniversary
Edition, 2008

Rhonda Byrne, *The Secret*, 2007

Lynne Cockrum-Murphy, *Stronger at the Broken Places: Heuristic Inquiry Growing Up in Chaos and the Journey from Suffering to Self-Actualization*, 2010

Howard Glasser, *You Are Oprah – Igniting the Fires of Greatness*, 2011

Louise Hay, *You Can Heal Your Life*, 1984

Elisabeth Haich, *Initiation*, 1965

Jack Kornfield, *A Path with Heart*, 1993

Jack Kornfield, *After the Ecstasy, the Laundry*, 2000

Thich Nhat Hanh, *Living Buddha, Living Christ*, 1996

Thich Nhat Hanh, *No Mud, No Lotus*, 2014

Ken Keyes Jr., *Handbook to Higher Consciousness*, 1976

Richard Matheson, *What Dreams May Come*, 1978 (released in film 1998)

Dan Millman, *The Life You Were Meant to Live*, 2010

Andrew Newberg and Mark Robert Waldman, *How God Changes Your Brain*, 2009

Ruth Stafford Peale, *The Adventure of Being a Wife*, 1971

Inna Segal, *The Secret Language of Your Body*, 2010

Swami Rama, *Living with the Himalayan Masters*, 2009

James Redfield, *The Celestine Prophecy*, 1993

Jane Roberts, *Seth Speaks*, 1994

Sanaya Roman and Duane Packer, *Opening to Channel,* 1993

Sanaya Roman, *Spiritual Growth: Being Your Higher Self,* 1992

Vianna Stibal, *Advanced ThetaHealing® Harnessing the Power of All That Is,* 2011

Doreen Virtue, *Archangels and Ascended Masters*, 2003

Book Club Discussion Questions:

1. Did *Living Hope – Steps to Leaving Suffering Behind* make you reflect on your life and your choices that brought you to where you are today? In what way? Did you reevaluate or confirm the things you thought were important?

2. What passages or chapters in particular resonated with you? Which struck you—personally—as most profound or meaningful for your own life?

3. Why is it that *Living Hope –Steps to Leaving Suffering Behind* has struck such a chord with people? Journalist Adriane Hopkins says it is because the book tells "a profound journey of discovery ... that readers can relate to and take away a sense of personal growth... in themselves as well". Do you agree? Are there any other reasons?

4. *Living Hope –Steps to Leaving Suffering Behind* offers general advice such as seek, be malleable, and question, along with providing lists of actions, films and books. Which, if any, of the tips struck you as most helpful? If so, in what way(s)?

5. Did you try any of the recommendations in the book; the activities, the Being/Doing chart, see films or read any other books? If so, what impact did it have on you?

6. As people hear about *Living Hope – Steps to Leaving Suffering Behind* they may be tempted to give the book to someone who has experienced trauma or abuse or substance abuse hoping it will guide them. What would you say to them? Do you think it will it help?

7. What kind of wisdom does this book offer about the importance and meaning of life?

*9 7 8 1 6 2 7 4 7 1 4 7 3 *